# 1 9 5 8 - 2 0 0 8

## 50 YEARS

## COLUMBUS STATE

### U N I V E R S I T Y

"For truly, Columbus College was conceived in community desire, was born through community endeavor, was nurtured during its youth by community care, was started on its college career with community expectations, and will be graduated as a full-grown institution in September 1966, with community joy and praise. Yes, this community is proud of its child, thankful to those who have helped it grow, and confidently entrusts it to those in whose hands it now rests. May it continue to enrich the life of the community by educating ever increasing numbers of fine young women and men…"

**J.Q. Davidson**
**Columbus College Commencement Address, June 7, 1965**

# *Enriching Lives:*
# A Pictorial History of
# Columbus State University

by Reagan L. Grimsley

*This volume is dedicated to the students, alumni, faculty, staff, and community members who participated in the development and growth of Columbus College, now Columbus State University, from 1958 to 2008. You are the heart and soul of the university.*

The Donning Company Publishers
184 Business Park Drive, Suite 206
Virginia Beach, VA 23462-6533

Steve Mull, General Manager
Barbara Buchanan, Office Manager
Wendy Nelson, Editor
Chad Casey, Graphic Designer
Derek Eley, Imaging Artist
Scott Rule, Director of Marketing
Lynn Walton, Project Research Coordinator

**B. L. Walton Jr., Project Director**

LIBRARY OF CONGRESS CATALOGING-IN-PUBLICATION DATA

GRIMSLEY, REAGAN L.
ENRICHING LIVES : A PICTORIAL HISTORY OF COLUMBUS STATE UNIVERSITY / BY REAGAN L. GRIMSLEY.
    P. CM.
INCLUDES BIBLIOGRAPHICAL REFERENCES AND INDEX.
1. COLUMBUS STATE UNIVERSITY--HISTORY. 2. COLUMBUS STATE UNIVERSITY--HISTORY--PICTORIAL WORKS. I. TITLE.
LD1273.G75 2008
378.771'57--DC22

2007048470

978-1-57864-494-0

# Contents

6     Foreword by Dr. Frank Douglas Brown

8     Preface

9     Acknowledgments

10     Chapter One: Columbus's Junior College

30     Chapter Two: A New and Growing Campus

58     Chapter Three: New Leadership, New Challenges

74     Chapter Four: To University Status and Beyond

108     Bibliography

110     Appendix I: Original Columbus College Faculty

111     Appendix II: First Graduating Class of Columbus College

112     Appendix III: Award-Winning Alumni, Faculty, Staff, and
             Students

119     Appendix IV: Emeriti Faculty

123     Index

128     About the Author

# Foreword

If ever a community longed for a college, Columbus, Georgia, was that city. For years before it became a reality, Columbus College, later Columbus State University, was coveted, dreamed of, and planned. Perhaps no other institution of higher education has ever been so anticipated, for so long, by so many!

Funds were collected to secure property for "the college" as early as the 1940s. Local leaders besieged state officials on the topic, and finally, in 1958, the Board of Regents authorized the creation of the school. Its beginnings were humble. An abandoned hosiery mill, with renovations, was its first home. But its spirit was always proud. It is not uncommon in Columbus today to encounter people from all walks of life who quickly claim the heritage of the Shannon Hosiery Mill experience.

The quality of our academic offerings and the dedication of the faculty and staff were hallmarks from the start, even when the facilities were modest. The relocation of the college to its present site in 1963 was the signal that higher education had found a home in Columbus.

The complete story of this university cannot be told, in pictures or otherwise, without a clear depiction of the town-and-gown cooperation that has so energized CSU from its beginnings. After giving birth to the college, the community continued to provide the financial and spiritual nurturing that has permeated this relationship since before its founding. Today, the university is paying rich dividends on that investment.

If a picture is truly worth a thousand words, this book will speak volumes about the institution we call ours. I hope you enjoy this extraordinary story of a community and its college, a story for the ages—a living story of yesterday, today, and, most importantly, tomorrow.

Frank Douglas Brown

Dr. Frank Douglas Brown, president of Columbus State University, 1988–2008

# Preface

Through images and narrative text, this book details how, over a span of fifty years, a small junior college located in a vacant mill with several hundred students blossomed into a state university with an enrollment of more than seventy-five hundred. This gradual transformation impacted the lives of thousands of people. Students who once roamed the halls, faculty who lectured to capacity classrooms, and the staff who kept the institution running smoothly in good and bad times all conjure reminiscences of campus life. Likewise, members of the community witnessed firsthand, and countless numbers actively took part in, the birth, adolescence, and maturity of the college. This volume hopes to rekindle those memories and ignite the flame of discovery for all those who seek to learn about the past of Columbus State.

A cumulative history of CSU is much needed, as no book-length volume documents the birth and growth of the university. Shorter pieces that illuminate the history of the college do exist and helped lay the groundwork for this volume. From 1983 through his retirement in 2001, Dr. Craig Lloyd worked to interpret the history of the college by penning several lengthy pieces including a booklet for the Twenty-Fifth Anniversary Celebration of Columbus College, and a history of the Columbus State University Foundation. His work also includes a journal article on the early life of the college, which provides analysis of the college in its youth. Dr. Lloyd's extensive research notes, located in the Columbus State University Collection at the Columbus State University Archives, were of great assistance in filling gaps in the college record. Dr. John Lupold's work *Columbus, Georgia: 1828-1978* places the founding and growth of the college in context with public education in the city in general, and his interpretation

was quite valuable in unraveling the complicated founding and establishment of Columbus College. Beyond these works, however, very little interpretive literature exists to tell the story of the college. While thin on secondary sources, primary sources that document the life of the college are abundant. Photographs, oral histories, the college annuals *Grey and Gold* and *Sentry,* the college newspaper *Saber,* and the textual records of the college offer a rich and vibrant portrait of collegiate life. The fiftieth anniversary of the founding of Columbus College offered the perfect opportunity to meld these sources into a book-length work that documents campus culture. This work is not intended, however, to be a comprehensive or definitive history of Columbus State University, a task which will be left to future scholars. Instead, *Enriching Lives* is a pictorial history of the growth and development of Columbus College, now Columbus State University, from its inception in 1958 through the first decade of the twenty-first century.

# Acknowledgments

Any author accrues debts in the course of his or her work, and I am no exception. First of all, this volume would not have been possible without the support of Dr. Frank Brown, president of Columbus State University. His support of this project, initiated in conjunction with the celebration of Columbus State University's fiftieth anniversary, was unwavering. The Columbus State University Foundation, under the guidance of executive director Dr. Lon Marlowe, provided funding for *Enriching Lives*. Dean Callie McGinnis of the Columbus State University Libraries championed the idea of a commemorative pictorial history, and her encouragement during all phases of the work was greatly appreciated. Bill Sutley of CSU Public Relations provided assistance in locating photographs and provided editorial advice on a number of occasions. The editorial board of Ray Lakes, John Lester, Dr. John Lupold, Dr. Lindsey Mock, and Geri Regnier read the work for content and historical accuracy, although I ultimately must take responsibility for any errors or omissions found in the work.

Others contributed to the book in various ways. The staff of the CSU Archives went far beyond prescribed duties in assisting with the research process. Giselle Bratcher offered support when I needed it most; Dalton Royer identified photographs and helped with obscure research questions; Megan Wilson and Morgan Carraway transcribed oral histories with key university alumni, faculty, and staff; and Sean Norman spent afternoons at the photocopier. Schwob Library staff member Martha Ragan created a splendid university timeline and assisted with tracking down hard-to-find details that greatly strengthen the content. Instructional Technology Services staff member Jon Haney also contributed with various research and technical tasks, and for his help I am particularly grateful. Virginia Causey's Spring 2007 oral history class contributed by conducting oral history interviews with key figures, and I would be remiss if their efforts in preserving the historical memory of our institution went unnoticed. Through their prior research and written works on the history of the university, retired history professors Dr. John Lupold and Dr. Craig Lloyd offered answers to my questions about the history of the university, and I only hope that my interpretation meets their exacting standards. Terri Kimble, a CSU alumna, edited the text, provided feedback on the early drafts, and contributed several photographs that add to the luster of this volume. Last but not least, Bernie Walton and Heather Floyd at the Donning Company are to be commended for their efforts to bring this history of Columbus State to life in book form.

The images included in this volume, unless otherwise noted, are work for hire by employees or contractors of Columbus College or Columbus State University. The majority are located in the Columbus State University Archives, Instructional Technology Services, or the Public Relations office. Thank you for contributing these incredible images of Columbus State University.

Reagan L. Grimsley

# Chapter One Columbus's Junior College

*"...the philosophy of the junior college is that the community and college are one."*
Thomas Y. Whitley, Columbus College President, oral history interview, November 19, 1982

When the doors to the Shannon Hosiery Mill opened on September 22, 1958, the line of people who steadily filed in were not textile workers reporting for their morning shift at the mill, but instead the first eager students at the newly minted Columbus College. As Peggy Watford registered for courses that Monday, she became the first student at a public educational institution that owed its very existence to the perseverance and determination of the local residents. Envisioned as a college to serve the post-secondary educational needs of Muscogee County and the greater Chattahoochee Valley, the new college would immediately begin enriching the lives not only of its cohort of new students, but the entire community.

Peggy Watford, a graduate of Jordan High School, is the first student to register for classes. Philip Battle and Glen Herrin, seated, are on hand to assist with the first registration.

The first class of Columbus College forms a line to register for classes on Monday, September 22, 1958.

Founded in 1828 as a trading town on the fall line of the Chattahoochee River, Columbus developed during its first century of existence into one of the leading municipalities in the state. The town represented one of Georgia's key urban areas in both population and economic influence. Although cotton reigned as king in the agricultural hinterlands of the city for a full century, the river city also developed key industries, such as textile manufacturing and iron foundries. The roaring water that spilled over the falls of the Chattahoochee provided power for the growing industrial concerns, especially the city's textile mills, which proliferated in the aftermath of the Civil War. A burgeoning New South urban area, Columbus enjoyed a reputation as a city friendly to industrial development. As the city entered the twentieth century, industry was not the only area in which it progressed. The new century brought about important changes in city services that impacted residents' quality of life, including professional fire and police departments, a new sewer system, a city-owned water works, and improvements in roads and bridges. This progressive attitude extended to the arena of education as well.

The growth of public education in Columbus followed the pattern of many other southern cities. Few educational opportunities existed in the city in the antebellum era, especially for the public. After the Civil War, Columbus opened its first public school system in 1867, and by 1872 Muscogee County offered public school education as well. As the twentieth century dawned, the city embarked on a number of initiatives to enhance public education. In 1905, the municipality was the first in Georgia to offer free kindergarten, and the Columbus School Board supported projects to build both a state-of-the-art vocational school, which debuted in 1906, and a Carnegie public library that greeted its first visitors in 1907. Historian John Lupold contends that "in the 1920s the city's schools were excellent, particularly when compared to the average educational system of the South." (Lupold, p.107) Despite

these achievements, by the beginning of the Second World War, no institution of higher education, either public or private, had put down roots deep enough to persist in the city.

The economic development generated by World War II prompted local leaders to seek ways to continue to improve Columbus, and in particular to institute a group that could publicly address specific civic needs. According to a speech delivered by William Henry Shaw in 1963, the origins of the movement for an institution of higher education in Columbus date to 1943. On October 13, 1943, Harry L. Williams, Theodore J. McGee, Walter A. Richards, and George C. Woodruff met to compose a letter in which they proposed a "Greater Columbus Committee" to study a wide variety of community issues. As the call for the formation of this body gained strength, twenty-two local citizens signed on in support of the project. By January 1944, the Columbus Chamber of Commerce, under the leadership of President J. Q. Davidson, endorsed the project as well. The result of this outpouring of community support was the Columbus Planning Association, Inc., which in April 1944 took on the role of examining and making recommendations on a number of pressing issues in the city. The new corporation set up nine committees: transportation, utilities, real estate and housing, business development, religious and social welfare, health, governmental agencies, schools, and area planning.

The special committee on schools later became the Committee on Education chaired by Roland Daniel. Other members of this committee included Paul Munro, Robert Arnold, Wimberley Jenkins, Clinton Moon, Mrs. J. E. Flowers, Mrs. Willis Battle, John Kinnett, and Maurice Rothschild. By 1945, this committee announced two important goals: consolidation of the city and county schools and the establishment of a junior college.

In the same year, William Henry Shaw came to Columbus to interview for the position of superintendent of the Columbus City Schools. During this interview, Board of Education members specifically addressed these same two goals, stating that the board desired to merge the city and county schools and seek the creation of a junior college to serve the county. The school board offered Shaw the position of superintendent, and he quickly went to work to achieve the tasks set before him. The consolidation of the city and county school districts would be achieved when the two successfully merged in 1950, while a number of local groups, including the Columbus City Schools, Muscogee County Schools, the Chamber of Commerce, and the City of Columbus, worked together in the interim to lay the groundwork for the proposed junior college. Finding an adequate site for the new post-secondary facility was of utmost importance. Prospective sites at the Columbus Country Club and the "Hatcher Tract" along the eastern side of Hilton Avenue did not materialize, but in December 1946 Mr. and Mrs. Walter L. Miller offered to sell their dairy farm located near Warm Springs Road and Cody Road as a site for the future college. Urban planners contended that the site, then on the northeastern fringe of the city, was particularly well suited for a college because of its location in an area projected to be highly developed in the coming decades. With a potential offer in hand, local leaders moved to raise both public awareness of the project and to secure funding. By the summer of 1947, Superintendent Shaw was able to secure a one-year option for the purchase of the dairy farm.

Meanwhile, in 1948 the Chamber of Commerce appointed a special committee to work toward obtaining the Miller farm. J. Q. Davidson served as chair of the committee, and other committee members included Robert M. Arnold, president of the Board of Education; Walter A. Richards, mayor; T. G. Reeves, chairman of the Commissioners of Roads and Revenues of Muscogee County; and William Henry Shaw, superintendent of education for the Columbus Public Schools. Still, no funding or governmental authority existed that would allow the group to move forward with the purchase, so in August 1948 the Millers allowed an extension of the purchase option for an additional year.

Despite these positive developments, those seeking to found a college in the county faced difficult obstacles. First, no funds existed to purchase the Miller site, and second, the state had not authorized the founding of a college. Not to be deterred, a group of citizens including J. Q. Davidson, T. G. Reeves, Walter A. Richards, Jack B. Key, Andrew Prather, Robert M. Arnold, Maurice D. Rothschild, and William H. Shaw met at Davidson's home on December 1, 1948, to plan for a fundraising reception in support of the new college. The reception, held at the Columbus Country Club on December 10, 1948, and attended by approximately fifty guests, was a formal call for donations to assist with the purchase of the Miller tract of land for a college. Showing their dedication to both post-secondary education and the idea of a junior college through the reception and subsequent efforts, more than 180 community subscribers raised more than ninety-two thousand dollars to be used to purchase the future college site. Although the money was now in hand to fund the purchase, the state legislature had not yet approved any local government entity to operate a college. This problem was cleverly solved through the Enabling Act of 1949, which authorized the merger of the Columbus Public Schools and the Muscogee County Schools and also included stipulations that the new Muscogee County School District would have the oversight of kindergartens, grade schools, high schools, colleges, and public libraries. Passed on February 25, 1949, Law Number 251 paved the way not only for a unified and more efficient public school system in the county, but also allowed the college project to move forward with the blessing of the state government.

The first consolidated Muscogee County School Board is sworn
in on January 2, 1950, by Judge T. Hicks Fort. The Muscogee
County School District and the Columbus City Schools merged
into the Muscogee County School District in 1950. Pictured
in the back row, left to right, are J. Q. Davidson, W. H. Moon,
and Walter A. Richards. Pictured in the front row, left to right,
are Mrs. J. Madden Hatcher, B. H. Hardaway, Jr., Mrs. Richard
Chaplin, W. C. Woodall, J. Stacey Jones, Louis Kunze, George
Adams, Dr. Guy Dillard, John Kinnett, and Mrs. Forbes Bradley.
(Photograph by Elmer Fink)

J. Q. Davidson takes the oath of office from Judge T. Hicks Fort
as a member of the Muscogee County School Board. Davidson
was a lifelong advocate for education, serving on numerous
committees for both secondary and post-secondary education.

In 1949 and 1950, the Board of Education purchased the Miller site, along with additional land held by Charlie Frank Williams and Lloyd Bowers, Sr., as the permanent site for a college. The total acreage of the combined sites slightly exceeded 157 acres. Work crews extended basic utilities including water and sewer lines to the campus site in 1949, and in 1953 the voters of Muscogee County affirmed a bond issue allocating one hundred thousand dollars for the construction of roads on the junior college campus. Through these actions, the city and county governments showed their commitment to establishing a postsecondary institution in Columbus.

William Henry Shaw served as superintendent of the Columbus City Schools from 1946–1950 and of the Muscogee County School District from 1950–1973.

During the early to mid-fifties, the struggle to found a college in Columbus continued. The establishment of the University of Georgia Extension Center at Jordan High School complicated the fight. Established in 1947, the center attracted local students seeking credits that could be transferred to four-year colleges in the state. The success of the University of Georgia Center was a double-edged sword: by the mid-1950s, seven hundred students were enrolled at the center, both highlighting the need for a post-secondary educational center and providing a competitor for any new college development. Two reports, one local and one statewide, would validate the fact that the area was ripe for the development of a junior college. Published in 1955 and issued by the Board of Regents of the University System of Georgia, the Junior College Study Report found that junior colleges were needed to offer higher education opportunities to residents, and that these junior colleges should be established across the state under the purview of the Board of Regents of the University System of Georgia. The

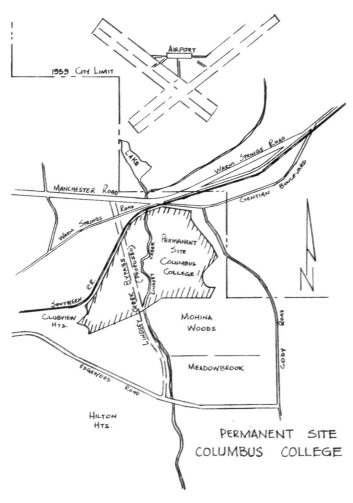

An early diagram of the permanent site of Columbus College.

second study report, compiled by the George Peabody College for Teachers, occurred from March 15, 1956, until March 15, 1957. While the task of this report was a comprehensive study of the Muscogee County School District, the committee also recommended that the school district support the establishment of a junior college in the county. These two reports both pointed toward the need for educational opportunities for local residents beyond the secondary school level.

As the move to establish a junior college gained momentum, the Board of Education of Muscogee County established the Junior College Committee consisting of chairman J. Q. Davidson and members B. H. Hardaway, Jr., John R. Kinnett, Sr., Walter A. Richards, William H. Shaw, Malcolm Forte, Frank Phillips, B. F. Register, Robert T. Davis, W. Ford Pearce, Thomas G. Moore, A. C. Briley, Jr., William Buck, W. H. Glenn, R. E. Martin, Jr., Mrs. Joseph Spano, Mrs. Sam Wilson, A. M. Pickard, J. Gordon Young, Forbes Bradley, and W. D. Swift. A committee of the Chamber of Commerce also formed, and by early 1958 J. Q. Davidson found himself in the position of chair of this body as well. A longtime supporter of a college in Columbus, Davidson consistently fought for local access to higher education. During 1957 and 1958, he led one or both committees, a daunting task for any leader, but one in which Davidson excelled. His efforts would soon come to fruition, but not without a number of twists and turns along the way.

By the fall of 1957, a movement to create a system of state-controlled junior colleges across the state was underway. In addition to the long sought-after college in Columbus, both Augusta and Savannah desired to have their locally administered junior colleges transferred to state supervision. In March 1957, the Georgia General Assembly gave Governor Marvin Griffin the power to appoint a special legislative committee to investigate the feasibility of establishing a junior college system in the Peach State.

On November 11, 1957, the committee journeyed to Columbus for a meeting on the direction of post-secondary education in Muscogee County. Both the Education Committee of the Chamber of Commerce, chaired at the time by Ford Pearce, and the Muscogee County Board of Education met with the group of six representatives from the Legislative Committee. In a concerted effort, each outlined the need for a college in Columbus and voiced their support for the establishment of an institution of higher education.

Among the members of the Legislative Committee was a young state senator from Augusta, Carl E. Sanders. Sanders played a unique role in the early growth of Columbus College. He was not only part of a legislative committee that studied the feasibility of establishing a college in Columbus, but once it was established, he pushed for the expansion of the college to four-year status during his term as governor of Georgia from 1963 to 1967. Two other local leaders also held statewide positions, which helped the junior college movement gain momentum. Board of Regents of the University System members Allen Woodall, Sr. and Howard "Bo" Callaway both advocated the need for a new junior college in the area, and their influence as members of the Regents certainly helped shape opinion in favor of placing a new institution in Columbus.

T. Hiram Stanley, William H. Shaw, and J. Q. Davidson were instrumental in the founding and early development of Columbus College. (Photograph courtesy of Nechtman Studio, Columbus, Georgia)

By January 1958, a group of diehard Columbusites had spent over a decade in the pursuit of a college in the city. Although a groundswell of public support occurred in late 1957, the report published in January 1958 by the Junior College Study Committee generated further excitement in the city. The report recommended that the state should appropriate money to support junior colleges in the state and that the Board of Regents of the University System of Georgia should be the governing body of these institutions. Action on the recommendations was swift, and the event that ultimately led to the founding of Columbus College occurred on February 20, 1958, when Bill 686, commonly known as the Junior College Act of 1958, successfully passed the Georgia legislature and became law with the signature of Governor Marvin Griffin. A group of seventeen Columbus residents journeyed to Atlanta to witness the signing of the bill, which provided state funds in support of operating costs in the amount of three hundred dollars per student.

Local leaders, anticipating the passage of the Junior College Act, were working to obtain a temporary site for the college by late January. Sensing the urgency of securing a charter and funding for a new junior college, local leaders announced the intent to establish a college in the city by September 1958. Since it would not be possible to construct a college campus on the east Columbus land by that fall, the school board instead selected the recently closed Shannon Hosiery Mill as the initial site for the college. On January 28, 1958, the Muscogee County Board of Education signed a thirty-day purchase option on the site, and on February 28, 1958, the contract became final when the board purchased the site for $250,000.

The intent in the first months of 1958 was for the Muscogee County School Board to fund, equip, and operate the new institution, but by April a new and more lucrative scenario evolved. The school board would provide a site and buildings on the Miller Dairy site by January 1, 1960, in exchange for the Board

of Regents of the University System approving the establishment of a junior college in Columbus and assuming supervision of its operations. Local leaders saw this as a financial boon—they would gain a Regents system institution without having to pay ongoing operating costs. With this agreement in hand on May 14, 1958, the Board of Regents of the University System of Georgia established a new junior college in Columbus as its seventeenth unit. Although the junior college bill prompted the creation of the college, it entered life as a new institution of the Board of Regents, not under the auspices of the Junior College Act of 1958.

The summer of 1958 was a whirlwind of activity as the Muscogee County Board of Education, the Board of Regents, and the new college administration all worked to ensure that the new facility would be in operation by the fall of 1958. Immediately after the founding of the college, Dr. Thomas Y. Whitley, then a special assistant working for the Regents System, became the first president by authority of the board. Born in Irwin County in 1916, Whitley earned his bachelor's and master's degrees from the University of Georgia, followed by a doctoral degree at the University of Texas. Before his brief stint with the Board of Regents of the University System of Georgia, Whitley served as dean at South Georgia College in Douglas, Georgia. His course of study at the doctoral level and experience in junior college administration, along with his Georgia roots, made him an ideal choice as the first president of the fledgling college. After his appointment, Whitley packed his bags for Columbus and went to work creating a college out of a defunct hosiery mill. By July, a renovation project budgeted at more than one hundred thousand dollars was underway at the Shannon vMill.

Two other critical events occurred during that summer. First, on May 29, 1958, the voters of Muscogee County overwhelmingly passed a school bond issue providing six million dollars for various school building projects in the county. Of this amount, one million dollars was earmarked to fund the construction of buildings on the permanent college campus site, formerly the Miller Dairy. While

Thomas Y. Whitley, the first president of Columbus College, served in that capacity from 1958 through 1979.

The Shannon Hosiery Mill served as the temporary home of Columbus College from September 1958 through December 1962. This image depicts the outside of the mill as it appeared in 1958.

the focus of the bond issue was not the new junior college, the passage of the act ensured that the school board would have the funds to complete the building project to which they had earlier agreed. It also underscored the commitment of the county's citizens to provide quality education to children and adults of all levels. The second major event of the summer occurred two weeks later, when on June 10, 1958, the Board of Regents officially named the new junior college Columbus College.

Refurbishing the mill into a college was only part of creating a new institution of higher learning. President Whitley oversaw the hiring of faculty and staff, the creation of a core curriculum, and the recruitment of students for the nascent college. As September drew nigh, fourteen faculty members and five administrative staffers joined the president as the first employees of Columbus College. Some of the newcomers would serve only one year, but others, such as Philip Battle, Katherine Mahan, Kenneth Nance, and Mary Livengood, would remain with the college until retirement, serving the college for decades to come. All, however, shared in the joy of welcoming nearly two hundred freshmen to registration on Monday, September 22, 1958.

During the first week at the new college, freshman students registered, underwent testing, and attended a variety of orientation programs. Sophomore students registered on September 29, 1958, and fall quarter classes met for the first time the same day. Fees for attendance for the fall quarter were thirty-nine dollars, which

This floor plan of the temporary site is for your use in orienting yourself to the building. The Administrative Offices are in the front of the building, opening off Talbotton Road. Facilities for Physical Education will be provided at the rear and side of the building.

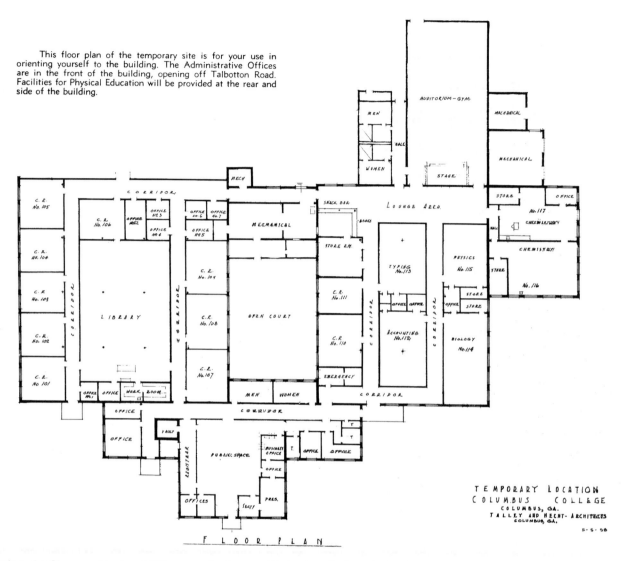

TEMPORARY LOCATION
COLUMBUS COLLEGE
COLUMBUS, GA.
TALLEY AND HECHT- ARCHITECTS
COLUMBUS, GA.
5-5-58

FLOOR PLAN

After renovation, the Shannon Hosiery Mill became the home of Columbus College in the fall of 1958. This floor layout oriented the students to their new college.

included a thirty-dollar matriculation fee, a three-dollar student welfare fee, and a six-dollar student activity fee. Classes during the fall quarter met five days per week, with seven class periods per day. First period began at 8:30 a.m., and the seventh period terminated at 3:55 in the afternoon. The school was organized by departments: business, education, fine arts, home economics, language, physical education, science and mathematics, and social sciences.

Orientation in 1958 wasn't all work. Here, freshmen Alton Russell, Margaret Wilson, Tommy Taylor, and Melanie Parkman chat during a break in the busy schedule.

On October 5, 1958, from 3:00 p.m. until 6:00 p.m., a special program took place to present Columbus College formally to the public. Having finally achieved their goal of opening a college in Columbus, the Columbus Chamber of Commerce and the Board of Education of the Muscogee County School District played a primary role in the celebratory grand opening ceremony. On hand for the ceremony were numerous local officials as well as Dr. Harmon W. Caldwell, chancellor of the Board of Regents; Robert O. Arnold, chairman of the Board of Regents; J. H. Dewberry, director of plant and business operations of the Board of Regents; and Board of Regents members Howard "Bo" Callaway and Morris M. Bryan, Jr. All were impressed with the transformation of the facility from textile mill into college. In an interview with local reporters that appeared in the October 6, 1958 Columbus Ledger, Chancellor Caldwell praised the newly renovated facilities: "The last time I was here, this was still an old hosiery mill. It's really

unbelievable to see these changes in four or five months. They have done a marvelous job."

While the community celebrated, J. Q. Davidson stressed that the community should remain focused on the creation of a permanent college campus. After sharing a list of thirty-one historical facts about the development of the college in the printed grand opening program, Davidson wrote:

THE COLUMBUS CHAMBER OF COMMERCE

and

THE BOARD OF EDUCATION
MUSCOGEE COUNTY SCHOOL DISTRICT

PRESENT

## COLUMBUS COLLEGE

"Community Service"

UNIVERSITY SYSTEM OF GEORGIA

3:00 P.M. — 6:00 P.M.

October 5, 1958

1338 Talbotton Road

Columbus, Georgia

The community welcomed the new college with a special program on October 5, 1958. This event celebrated the opening of Columbus College, an institution that local citizens, the Columbus Chamber of Commerce, the Muscogee County School District, and the City of Columbus worked tirelessly to attain.

"The foregoing historical facts show the realization of a community dream in the establishment of Columbus College. However, this is just the beginning. We must now work to have the permanent college site ready for occupancy in September, 1960. While the Muscogee County Board of Education will take the lead in getting the site ready, they will need the active support of the community in working out the many problems which will arise. Let us now dedicate ourselves to the completion of this community project!"

Davidson's statement was on target, because it would be four years, not the estimated two, before the permanent location on Warm Springs Road opened.

J. Q. Davidson and Howard "Bo" Callaway were both early supporters of Columbus College.

The faculty, staff, and students of the new college soon settled into the day-to-day routine of college life. Despite the short length of preparatory time between the organization of the college and the arrival of the first students, not only academic life but also student activities blossomed. During the first year at the mill site, a student

government association, men's basketball team, glee club, dramatics club, and an athletic association organized. A college dance, the "Harvest Hop," held on November 1, 1958, was the first social event for the new college, and it gave the students a chance to interact outside the classroom. Proceeds from the dance went to support the entry of a Columbus College float in the Columbus Christmas Parade. In the spring, another dance, this one formal, was held at

Adelaide Betts, Miss Saber 1959, was also voted Most Beautiful by the first Columbus College class.

The first men's basketball team at Columbus College struggled to a 1-8 record. Bottom row, left to right: Lowell Armon, Larry Armon, Rudon Tuck, James Lane, Robert Burnett, Wade Munford, Al Smith (manager). Top row, left to right: Coach Frank Townsend, Jack Reynolds, Don Jenkins, Teddy Brostrom, Jack Schorr, Larry Rodgers, Jack Slayton, and Jim Nelson.

the Columbus Country Club on May 22, 1958. At the latter dance, the first Miss Saber, Adelaide Betts, was crowned. Not all the year's activities were as successful, however. The young basketball team struggled through the season, winning only one out of the nine games played. In spite of this setback in its initial year, it would not take long for the college to develop a solid athletics program.

As the fledgling college took shape, students also began work on a student newspaper and the first college annual. By November 1958, the school had official school colors, gold and grey, a team nickname, Rebels, and a name for the campus newspaper, *Saber*. Student Don Jenkins submitted the winning entries for the school colors and team name, while Malcolm Wallace submitted the winning entry for the student newspaper. Created during the era of segregation at an all-white school, these symbols of the Old South were popular college mascots in the southeast, and with the hundredth anniversary of the War Between the States looming, it was no surprise that the students selected a symbol of the former Confederacy as a mascot of the college. The Rebel would be one of the primary symbols of the college from 1958 until 1970, when a change in culture and climate deemed it necessary to retire the Rebel from use and introduce both new school colors and a new nickname.

The Rebel was the official mascot of Columbus College from 1958–1970. Shown in this picture are Bill Phillips, Rebel Mascot, along with Carolyn Jones, Lavern Green, Susan Goodroe, Robert Belknap, and Judy Harbuck

Don Jenkins receives a gift certificate from Mary Maddox for naming the Rebels and suggesting the school colors of gold and grey.

While college culture evolved at the Talbotton Road facility, the proposed construction of buildings on the permanent site on Warm Springs Road ground to a halt. The problem was the new construction of a north-to-south transportation artery, the Lindsay Creek Bypass. The preferred path for the new limited-access road would route it through the western end of the college property, separating roughly thirty acres of the main site. Although the original agreement with the Board of Regents of the University System of Georgia called for the campus to open in 1960, the uncertainty of the specific course of the bypass through the college campus created an almost two-year delay in the project. Instead of a completed campus by the fall of 1960, the Muscogee County School Board instead had merely approved plans for the construction of four buildings on the Warm Spring Road site. Construction did not begin on the first four college buildings until October 1961, and it would be January 1963 before the college could occupy the site. These delays extended the college's stay at the Shannon Mill site from two years to four-and-a-half years.

From 1958 until December 1962, the Shannon Hosiery Mill housed Columbus College as it grew and thrived. From an initial enrollment of fewer than three hundred students in the fall of 1958, by fall 1962 the number of students attending the college rose to 768. Several milestones occurred during this time period. In 1960, the faculty selected Carl Franklin as the first student to receive the Faculty Cup award. Presented annually to an outstanding and deserving Columbus College student, this award is the highest honor a student at the institution can receive.

Dr. Thomas Whitley and Dr. J. Wilson Comer hand out diplomas to members of the first graduating class on June 5, 1960. Graduate Judy Grimes happily accepts her degree.

Carl Franklin receives the first Faculty Cup award. The Faculty Cup continues to be the highest honor a student can receive at the institution.

The first commencement exercise was another important milestone for the entire college community. On Sunday, June 5, 1960, the first graduating class of students gathered in the Columbus College auditorium to receive the first degrees awarded by Columbus College. The commencement address, delivered by T. Hiram

Stanley, chairman of the board of Royal Crown Cola Company, the chairman of the College Committee of the Muscogee County Board of Education, and the chairman of the Columbus Chamber of Commerce, focused on the importance of education. Stanley extolled the worth of a college degree, stating, "In tomorrow's world of electronics and automation, in the wonder world which lies ahead, the opportunities are going to the young men and women who are eager for and determined to secure further training. This world of the future will obviously recognize that the most important asset

will be educated and mature individuals." As Stanley's prophetic words soaked in, thirty-one students received their diploma from administrators Dr. T. Y. Whitley and Dr. J. Wilson Comer.

A group of dedicated faculty prepared the students who graduated from Columbus College during the mill era. Several new faculty members arrived in the fall of 1959, along with a new dean, Dr. J. Wilson Comer. Comer's experience in higher education, which included nearly twenty years of service to Georgia College at Milledgeville, made him a solid choice for the job. Katherine Mahan taught music and advised the Glee Club and the Baptist Student Union, Philip Battle sponsored the Camera Club while serving as instructor in Spanish and social studies, and William Howard advised the student newspaper in addition to serving as a professor of English. In 1960, a youthful William C. LeNoir arrived on campus as an instructor in the biology department, beginning a career which

T. Hiram Stanley delivered the first commencement address at Columbus College. Stanley Hall is named in his honor.

J. Wilson Comer served as the first dean of Columbus College from June 1959 until June 1961, when he assumed the position of president at Abraham Baldwin Agricultural College.

Philip Battle, one of the original Columbus College faculty members, shows that he is a man of many talents. Battle would serve the college until his retirement in 1992.

would span more than three decades and eventually include service as the acting president of Columbus College. Many other members of the faculty and staff worked hard to ascertain that Columbus College students not only achieved academic excellence in the classroom but were able to take part in worthwhile extracurricular activities as well.

Although Frank Townsend made an admirable start to a program of physical education, the addition of Frank "Sonny" Clements and Mary V. Blackmon greatly strengthened the program. Taking over a basketball team that played a limited, nine-game schedule in 1958–1959 and won only one game, Clements guided the second-year Rebel squad to three wins and fourteen losses during its first season as a member of the Georgia Junior College Conference. The third year of men's basketball saw vast improvement, as the team won fifteen and lost only five for its first-ever winning season. This success continued into the 1961–1962 season, and the Rebels finished with sixteen wins versus six losses. By 1963–1964, the Columbus College hoopsters developed into a well-oiled machine, winning nineteen games and losing six, and meanwhile advanced to the finals of the Georgia Junior College Conference Tournament, where they lost to champion South Georgia.

Harper Lee, author of *To Kill a Mockingbird*, chats with Columbus College students in January 1961.

Frank "Sonny" Clements arrived at Columbus College in 1959, quickly instituting a baseball team and shaping the college basketball team into a winning program.

The first Columbus College baseball team won three games and lost eight. Members shown in this photograph include, kneeling left to right: Coach Frank "Sonny" Clements, Don Hamrick, Ken Spano, Peanut Dison, George Casion, Jim Lane, George Pate, Bill Brogdon, and Wade Munford. Standing, left to right, are Walter Jordan, manager, Charles Kelly, Brinson Battiato, Charles Smith, Inman Callihan, Lamar Holmes, Eddie Lammons, Ben Fant, Robert Burnett, and Hubert Hayes.

In addition to the early success in basketball, Coach Clements also organized the first Columbus College baseball team, which hit the field for the first time on April Fool's Day 1960 and came away with a win over Southern Technical College, 5–2. While the season ended with only three wins versus eight losses, the Rebels proved they could hold their own on the diamond in the Georgia Junior College Conference.

A third league sport, men's golf, debuted in 1960-1961 under the guidance of Dewey Cash. Golf would eventually become one of the most succesful sports at Columbus College.

While only a handful of students were able to take part in the three league sports, intramurals were also an important part of Columbus College life. As advisor of the intramural council, Mary V. Blackmon assisted with the organization of sporting competitions including bowling, volleyball, archery, swimming, tennis, and boxing. As the move to a permanent home loomed large in the fall of 1962, physical education at Columbus College was certainly off and running.

Mary V. Blackmon worked to ensure that physical education was top notch at the young college.

Although the Talbotton Road facility provided a quality home for the junior college, by the fall of 1962 the end of the mill era was nigh. Planning for the Lindsay Creek Bypass and construction delays on the first buildings at the new site postponed the transfer of the campus to the permanent site until January 1963. By December 1962, however, the faculty, staff, and students of Columbus College were packing boxes and moving equipment to their new campus

Columbus College at the Shannon Hosiery Mill location, 1960.

off of Warm Springs Road. Excitement reigned in both the college family and the community as the long-anticipated campus of Columbus College became a reality. In January 1963, the hopes and dreams of a community would come true as Columbus College, not yet five years old, would finally be able to call home the site purchased for it more than a decade earlier.

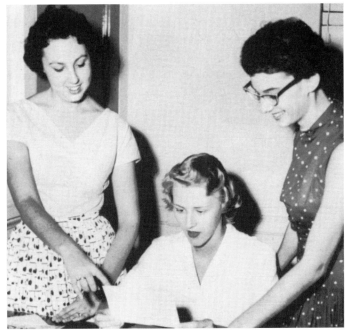

Members of the *Grey and Gold* staff review prospective content. Pictured are Nancy Langford, editor Eleanor Kirkpatrick, and Marlene Elmore.

The staff of the 1958–1959 annual, the *Grey and Gold*. In the back row, left to right, are Carl Franklin, Carson Melvin, Wayne Wilkes, Mary Moore, Lee Roe, Marilyn Gibson, and Clifford Born. The front row, left to right, consists of Nancy Langford, Marlene Elmore, Jo Ann Lawson, and Eleanor Kirkpatrick.

*"As children tired of playing,*
*At sunset hurry home,*
*Back to Columbus College,*
*We too shall someday come.*
*And when across our pathways,*
*Time's cool grey shadows fall,*
*You'll hear our weary footsteps*
*Returning to its halls.*
*To Columbus College—our alma mater,*
*Our Loyalty we give,*
*To be its pride and honor,*
*It taught us how to live."*

**Dedication of the 1958–1959** *Grey and Gold* **Annual**

Advisors William Howard and William Ryan with the staff of the 1960–1961 student newspaper. The *Saber* has published regularly since the fall quarter of 1958. Shown with Howard are Brenda Goodroe, editor Bobby Ledford, Arleen King, Janice Slayden, Etta Brown, Bill Clemmons, John Johnson, Gail Stephens, and Beth Hutchins.

Faculty members Alvin McLendon and William Howard look on as students Linda Skinner and Robert Belknap of the Fellowship Council prepare gift packages for the alms house to be distributed on Thanksgiving Day 1960.

Dr. T.Y. Whitley inspects damage done by a January ice storm at the Talbotton Road campus.

James Edmondson of the 1960–1961 Rebels dribbles for the camera.

Mr. and Miss Columbus College 1960–1961, sophomores Bill Brogdon and Carolyn Martin, were chosen based on their scholarship, character, and service.

Members of the Student Government Association undertake many projects to better inform the student body. Johnny Quick of the 1960 Student Government distributes information to Jimmy Blount and Carol Dyess on the 1960 Presidential race pitting John F. Kennedy against Richard Nixon.

Walter Jordan receives the first Columbus College letter sweater in 1960.

Robert Belknap and Susan Goodroe display their school spirit.

Registrar Mary Livengood answers questions for Elizabeth Hunter.

The Columbus College golf team made its debut in 1961. Faculty member Dewey Cash, left, and team members Ray Kinchen, Sammy Coolik, Bobby Cole, Jerry Sonich, and Ken Crumpler pose for the camera.

A young William C. LeNoir, Jr., joined the Columbus College faculty in 1960. LeNoir Hall is named in his honor.

One of the original Columbus College faculty members, Katherine Mahan served the college for more than three decades.

*"...we had a degree of closeness during the time we were in the mill, maybe it was partly because we were all under one roof, maybe it was partly because we were small, maybe it was because we were all working together for easily defined objectives...."*

Thomas Y. Whitley, oral history interview, December 6, 1982

# Chapter Two   A New and Growing Campus

*"I join all Georgians in congratulating Columbus College. The moving of this fine institution to a new campus is a fitting climax to the hard devoted efforts of the people of Columbus to provide higher education for the youth of Muscogee County and Georgia."*

*Telegram from Carl Sanders, Governor of Georgia, 1963–1967, to Columbus College, January, 1963*

On January 2, 1963, the Columbus College Rebels basketball team rang in the New Year and christened a new gymnasium at the same time, as the talented varsity squad handed their opponents, the Columbus College Alumni, an 81-65 defeat. The contest was the first true home game for both the varsity and the alumni team, as from 1958 through the fall of 1962 all Columbus College games took place either on the road or at the Columbus High gymnasium. Although the basketball team blossomed under the tutelage of Coach Clements, having a court to call their own was gratifying to the players, coaching staff, and the supporters of the program. The state-of-the-art sports facility also added to the prestige of the young program, which appeared in the 1962-1963 Georgia Junior College Conference title game and won conference titles in both 1963-1964 and 1964-1965. More importantly, the Wednesday night game was the first major event held on the new "permanent" campus of Columbus College, located on the former Miller Dairy site.

The 1962–1963 Columbus College Rebels finally gained a home with the construction of a gym on the Warm Springs Road campus. The team finished 21-8 and advanced to the title game of the Georgia Junior College Conference Tournament.

Coach Clements and his team celebrate winning the 1963–1964 Georgia Junior College Conference Championship. They would repeat as champions in 1964–1965.

The opening of the new college campus in January 1963 was a milestone event in the life of the institution, even though it came much later than originally planned. In 1958 the community boasted a college but still needed to transplant their young seedling to a spot where it could grow and prosper. Even without the delays caused by the routing of the Lindsay Creek Bypass through the western section of the campus site, the construction project was a complicated one. The college buildings required the stamp of approval of both the Board of Regents of the University System of Georgia and the Muscogee County School District before construction could begin. In 1960, the school board selected the Columbus firm J. N. Pease to design the original campus

structures. By 1961, the architectural plans were complete, and by late summer the final plans received the approval of the Muscogee County Board of Education. After accepting bids for the project in September 1961, the school board selected the firm of R. H. Wright, Jr. and Associates to construct the five initial buildings: a classroom building, an administration and library building, a physical education and student services building, a laboratory building, and a maintenance building. Work on the new campus began in earnest in October 1961, with the hope that the campus would be complete in time for 1962 fall quarter classes. As is not unusual with construction projects, the September 1962 deadline for occupation of the new

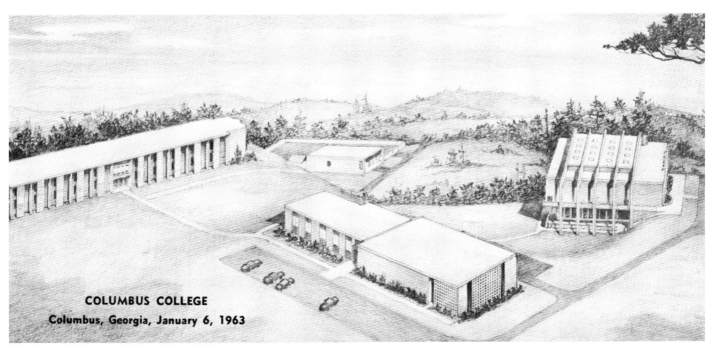

COLUMBUS COLLEGE
Columbus, Georgia, January 6, 1963

The four main buildings of the Columbus College campus include the classroom building, renamed Howard Hall; the administration/library building, renamed the Woodall Building; the gymnasium, renamed Woodruff Gym; and the laboratory building, renamed the Tucker Building.

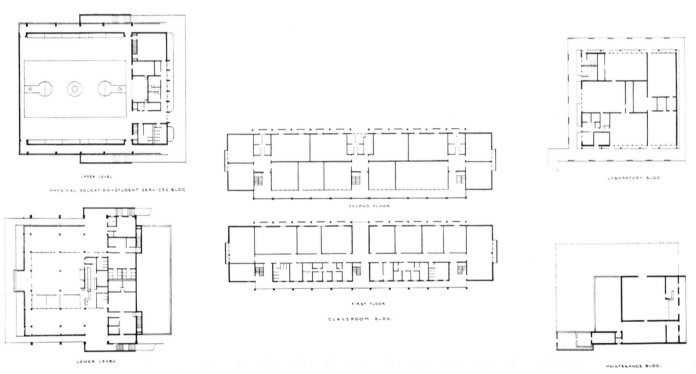

**COLUMBUS COLLEGE**
**Columbus, Georgia**

Constructed by Muscogee County Board of Education
Muscogee County School District, Columbus, Georgia

Presented to the Board of Regents
University System of Georgia
January 6, 1963

J. N. Pease and Company, Architects and Engineers
R. H. Wright, Jr., and Associates, Contractors

The floor plans for Columbus College campus buildings as they appeared in 1963.

site proved too ambitious, and it was not until December 1962 that the college began its move from the temporary quarters in the Shannon Hosiery Mill to its new home on Warm Springs Road in east Columbus. Lindsey Mock, then assistant dean of

students, recalled the transition between the two campuses in an oral history interview conducted in 2007: "Well, it was a lot of fun, but also a lot of work because we had a library to move. And you had all the furniture to move….everyone was so eager…."

Judging by the crowd on hand for the Formal Opening Program of the college site on January 6, 1963, it was not only those directly attached to the college but the entire community that was eager to celebrate the new college campus. A capacity crowd of twelve hundred people filed into the new gymnasium to participate in a two-hour program that included speeches by William Henry Shaw, superintendent of the Muscogee County School Board; Dr. Harmon W. Caldwell, chancellor of the University System of Georgia; Dr. Thomas Y. Whitley, president of Columbus College; John R. Kinnett, Sr., chairman of the property committee of the Muscogee County Board of Education; and Carl E. Sanders, governor-elect of the State of Georgia. T. Hiram Stanley, college chairman of the Muscogee County Board of Education, who played an integral role in the construction of the campus, served as master of ceremonies for the event. The Jordan Vocational High School band, under the direction of Robert M. Barr, and the Columbus College choir, under the direction of Katherine B. Mahan, added musical flair to the afternoon affair. Other participants included Dr. Fredrick S. Porter, who offered the invocation, and J. H. Dewberry, director of plant and building operations for the

University System of Georgia, who officially accepted the key for the new campus for the Board of Regents of the University System. B. H. Hardaway, president of the Muscogee County Board of Education, officially transferred the deeds to the campus and buildings from the Muscogee County School District to the Board of Regents of the University System of Georgia—the culminating event in a twenty-year campaign to both found a public college in Muscogee County and provide it with a proper home.

Dr. Harmon Caldwell delivers an address entitled "The History and Role of the University System" at the formal opening of Columbus College on January 6, 1963. (Photograph courtesy of Nechtman Studio, Columbus, Georgia)

John R. Kinnett, Sr., chairman of the property committee of the Muscogee County Board of Education, presents a key to Columbus College to J. H. Dewberry, director of plant and building operation of the Board of Regents of the University System of Georgia.

Professor Katherine Mahan and the Columbus College Choir of 1962–1963 performed at the formal opening ceremony.

After two decades of community activism in support of a college, the formal opening was indeed a dream realized, but at least one speaker saw an expanded role for Columbus College. In his speech, Governor-Elect Sanders, who in 1957 visited Columbus as a member of the junior college study committee, lauded the community for their dedication to higher education and promised that with the opening of the new campus, more Muscogee County natives could now study,

Carl E. Sanders, governor-elect of Georgia, speaks to a crowd of twelve hundred during the formal opening of Columbus College. Seated in the background is Dr. William Henry Shaw. (Photograph courtesy of Nechtman Studio, Columbus, Georgia)

graduate, and contribute to the community without ever leaving it. A strong proponent of education, Sanders also hinted that four-year status might not be far off for the college.

Indeed, after his inauguration as governor later in the month, Sanders made education a priority in his administration, calling for comprehensive planning to increase access to education in the Peach State. In 1963, Sanders created the Governor's Commission to Improve Education, designed to survey elementary, secondary, vocational-technical, and higher education in Georgia. This was the first comprehensive, statewide study of education in Georgia. The study noted that both long-range planning and an expansion of educational services to meet the needs of a changing economy were necessary. The study was indeed urgent for higher education, as the mid-sixties saw the arrival of the baby boom generation in college classrooms across the nation. In response to this influx of college students, Georgia created a series of new junior colleges across the state and granted four-year status to Augusta College, Armstrong Atlantic College, Georgia Southwestern College, and Columbus College. In 1963, Columbus College moved to a new campus, and true to Sanders' word, by 1964 the Board of Regents of the University System of Georgia gave the college permission to begin offering upper-level classes in 1968.

Governor-elect Sanders chats with Hazel Lewis and Dr. William Henry Shaw during the formal opening ceremonies at Columbus College in January 1963. (Photograph courtesy of Nechtman Studio, Columbus, Georgia)

The new campus came just in time for Columbus College. In the fall quarter of 1962, 768 students attended classes at the school. By 1975, that number swelled to 5,674. This increase can be attributed to a number of related factors, some national and some local in nature. First, the baby boom generation caused a dramatic increase in the number of college-age students nationwide. Second, the number of students seeking higher education, whether in support of career goals or to avoid military service in Vietnam, increased across the nation as well. A third contributing factor to the rapid increase in population at Columbus College was the shift in status from a two-year junior college to a four-year institution.

In 1968, the first year that upper-level classes were taught on the campus, fall enrollment was 1,810. The number surged to 3,245 by the fall quarter of 1970, one semester after the adolescent college awarded its first bachelor's degrees. Combined with the expansion of Fort Benning during this time period, the demand for college education in the region created student numbers that threatened to overwhelm both the physical facilities and the staff of the college.

Between the opening of the new campus in 1963 and late 1975, the student body grew at a phenomenal rate. In the mid-1960s, the college awarded some forty to fifty associate degrees yearly, but at the first baccalaureate graduation in 1970, 179 graduates received their bachelor's degrees in arts, science, and education. The college further expanded its educational offerings in the early 1970s, offering master's degree programs in education. In 1974, the college awarded its first master's degrees during the spring quarter graduation. The Southern Association of Colleges and Schools granted Columbus College accreditation in 1963, a major step in ensuring that education at the college was in line with other post-secondary institutions in the southeast. Accreditation, along with the subsequent expansion of the curriculum, made the college a solid choice for local residents who wanted to obtain a college degree but did not have the option of attending a university outside the Columbus area. While this helped fuel the growth of the college, it also sometimes hampered recruitment efforts. Since no dorms existed on the campus, the college was essentially a commuter school, and the nickname "Cody Road High" was often used to describe the college.

As the college grew, however, it came to look less and less like a high school and more like a true institution of higher education. To accommodate the needs of the expanding student body, new buildings went up on campus regularly and quickly. Only three years after the formal opening of the college, construction began on a new classroom building for the sciences as well as a new administration building, both of which opened in the fall of 1966. By 1969, the gymnasium expanded to include a pool, and both a student center and fine and performing arts building were also added to campus.

Until this time, the only named facility on campus was the Simon Schwob Memorial Library, housed in the first administration building. Letters of the alphabet designated other buildings. In 1969, a move was afoot to name the buildings on campus, and the Columbus College faculty, along with an ad hoc committee of citizens, established criteria for the persons for whom the buildings would be named and then made the selection. The Board of Regents of the University System of Georgia approved the building names, and on June 1, 1969, seven buildings on the Columbus College campus received new official names.

The original classroom building was renamed Howard Hall in honor of William Howard, one of the first faculty members of Columbus College who died in 1964. The original science building, then known as the biology building, was renamed the Tucker Building in honor of William C. Tucker, Sr., longtime editor of the *Columbus Enquirer-Sun*. The gymnasium, also one of the first corps of campus buildings, received the name Woodruff Gymnasium to honor the legacy of James W. Woodruff, Sr., a local philanthropist and businessman who worked to establish a series of locks and dams on the Chattahoochee River. The new science building, which opened in the fall of 1966, received the name Arnold Building in honor of Robert M. Arnold, a Columbus lawyer and longtime member of the Board of Trustees of the Columbus Public Schools. The administration building, which also opened in 1966, became the Richards Building in honor of former Columbus mayor and businessman Walter A. Richards. Richards worked in a variety of government capacities and served as a member of the first board of education of the consolidated Muscogee County Schools in 1950. The Davidson Building, the

The physical education building under construction, 1968.

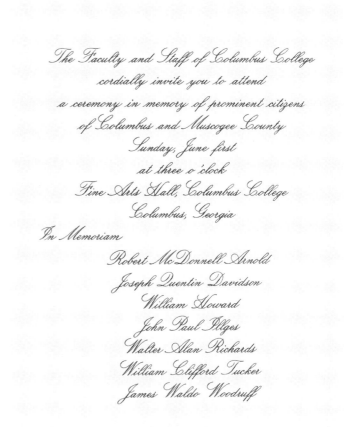

*The Faculty and Staff of Columbus College
cordially invite you to attend
a ceremony in memory of prominent citizens
of Columbus and Muscogee County
Sunday, June first
at three o'clock
Fine Arts Hall, Columbus College
Columbus, Georgia*

*In Memoriam*

*Robert McDonnell Arnold
Joseph Quentin Davidson
William Howard
John Paul Illges
Walter Alan Richards
William Clifford Tucker
James Waldo Woodruff*

The family of J. Q. Davidson received this invitation to the 1969 ceremony to rename seven campus buildings in memory of community leaders.

recently opened student services building, gained its name in honor of lawyer and longtime college advocate J. Q. Davidson. Finally, the proposed medical education building would be named in the honor of John P. Illges, a visionary business leader of the Columbus community. Serving as master of ceremonies, Jac H.

Rothschild noted that "the naming of these buildings for these seven community giants just confirms an epitaph—that you live in the hearts of those you leave behind—you never die." Today students are reminded of the legacy of these community leaders as they study, work, and play within the walls of these buildings.

By 1967, a growing campus greeted Columbus College students.

Two years after the ceremony, programs in nursing, dental hygiene, and medical technology occupied the Illges Health Science Building. The construction boom did not falter, however. By the fall of 1971, faculty from across campus moved into the newly minted Faculty Office Building. The Elizabeth Bradley Turner Center for Continuing Education began serving the community in 1974. With the student body still growing at a remarkable rate, in early 1975 the new $2.5-million Simon Schwob Memorial Library opened to provide expanded space for much-needed information and research materials, as well as a local history archive. May of 1975 saw the dedication of Stanley Hall, a one-million-dollar classroom building equipped with large, tiered lecture halls. The last building constructed in this era of

rapid expansion was Jordan Hall, and a January 1977 ceremony signaled that the new home for the education and business administration programs was ready for use. In a span of fourteen years, fifteen new edifices rose on the gently rolling hills of the campus, forever changing the young junior college into a mature institution with both undergraduate and graduate programs.

Although the state funded the construction of the vast majority of these buildings, two of the facilities were the direct effort of public support for the college. The construction of a new fine arts building and a facility for continuing education represented a significant trend for the college, as later buildings both on the main campus and the RiverPark campus in uptown Columbus would come to fruition only through a combination of

Industrialist Simon Schwob operated the Schwobilt Company in Columbus until his death in 1954 and was a supporter of the movement to erect a college in Columbus. The college placed this portrait of him in the Simon Schwob Memorial Library in 1963.

Students dedicated the 1967 yearbook to Ruth Schwob in honor of her many contributions to Columbus College.

funding from the local community and the college's foundation.

The construction of the fine arts building was in large part due to the fundraising ability of Ruth Schwob, widow of local industrialist Simon Schwob. At the time of his death in 1954, Simon Schwob willed fifty thousand dollars to a new college in Columbus if the facility opened within five years of his demise. On November 8, 1962, the Simon Schwob Foundation made good on this promise by presenting the college with a check for one hundred thousand dollars as a contribution to the building program. In January 1963, a ceremony took place to name the library, then located in the administration building, in honor of Simon Schwob.

With a keen interest in the arts, Ruth Schwob envisioned a program of excellence in this area at the college. She also convinced the college administration and the recently founded Columbus College Foundation to support her efforts. In a 1982 oral interview, Dr. T. Y. Whitley related, "In working with Mrs. Schwob, I became convinced that a strong music program was in the best interest of Columbus College. She was interested in improving the appreciation of art, music, and drama in the Columbus area, and I began to see that this was a way to definitely involve a great many more people in Columbus, and that the fine arts program, particularly the one in music, should serve as a very good window between the community and the college."

Schwob not only won over the college's president, but by June 1965, Schwob received authorization from the Columbus College Foundation to begin a fundraiser for the amount of five hundred thousand dollars to match state funds to build a new facility that would house the fine and performing arts. Working with donors large and small, Mrs. Schwob exceeded the goal. When matched by state and federal funds, she enabled the 1967 construction of the $1.25-million Fine Arts Hall. Dedicated in May 1969, the building also featured a dramatic sculptured

fountain designed by Richard Spence with a surrounding mosaic design of the academic muses by Wendell Taylor. In recognition of her outstanding efforts, the Columbus Business and Professional Women's Club named Mrs. Schwob the Woman of the Year for 1966, and in the same year she received the Service to Mankind Award from the Columbus Sertoma Club. Columbus College Professor Craig Lloyd summed up her vision in his 1983 work *Columbus College: Reaching for Tomorrow*, "Mrs. Schwob dared to dream and plan on a big scale." (Lloyd, *Reaching for Tomorrow*, p.4)

Fine Arts Hall opened in May 1969 and would house the fine and performing arts programs of the college until their relocation to the downtown campus in 2001 and 2007.

Like Fine Arts Hall, the establishment of the Elizabeth Bradley Turner Center for Continuing Education was a result of local support for the institution. Seeking funding for a building to house the continuing education programs regularly held on campus since 1962, Whitley approached local businessman D. Abbott Turner with the plans for a new facility. Although his intent was to build support for the program and seek matching funds from the Board of Regents, Whitley came away with an astounding promise from Turner: he would fund the entire million-dollar project in the memory of his recently deceased wife, Elizabeth Bradley Turner. Begun in July 1973, the new home for the Continuing Education Division of the college opened in November 1974. With classrooms, conference rooms, and office space, the Elizabeth Bradley Turner Center immediately began serving the community as a nexus of non-credit programming ranging from art to personal health. Once again, local philanthropy allowed the college to expand its educational offerings to a broader cross-section of the Columbus community.

In February 1979, a blanket of snow enveloped the Elizabeth Bradley Turner Center for Continuing Education.

Philanthropic efforts gave the institution much more than buildings, however. Seeking a group to promote private fundraising for the college, Whitley worked with Myron Greentree to heighten awareness of the need for such a group. A native Columbusite, Greentree then served as a member of the University of Miami's Foundation and was well aware of the benefits of having an organization to assist with funding for the college that the state could often not provide.

In August 1963, Greentree spoke to a select group of local residents about his experiences with college foundations and the positive influences just such a group could have on the life of students, faculty, and the community. Greentree suggested the need existed for a similar group at Columbus College. Local leaders acted with immediate resolve on his proposal, forming a steering committee to lay the groundwork for the Columbus College Foundation. Local attorney Howell Hollis prepared the original charter for the group, adopted on December 3, 1963. Designed "to promote the cause of higher education at Columbus College," the charter of the new Columbus College Foundation was to create scholarships and endowments and "do any or all things for the benefit of the educational activities of the college."

By early 1964, the first Columbus College Foundation Board of Trustees took office, a group that included Dr. Arthur N. Berry, Richard H. Bickerstaff, James W. Blanchard, Thomas Buck, Jr., Cason Callaway, Jr., Charles S. Daley, J. Q. Davidson, Wilbur H. Glenn, Myron Greentree, B. H. Hardaway III, Mrs. Ralph Hobbes, Mrs. J. P. Illges, Jr., Harry C. Jackson, G. Gunby Jordan II, Ms. T. K. Kendrick, John R. Kinnett, Sr., Jack Passailaique, Gerald B. Saunders, Henry Schwob, Allen M. Woodall, and James W. Woodruff, Jr. The board quickly organized an executive committee and began raising money in line with their goal of supporting the educational objectives of the college.

In his work *Their Time, Their Influence, Their Substance: The Story of the Columbus College Foundation, 1963–1993*, historian Craig Lloyd relates the many contributions of the foundation during this period, including faculty development grants, scholarships, equipment for critical college programs such as nursing, dental hygiene, and criminal justice, the purchase of properties adjoining the college campus, and support of the Learning Center and Tutorial Program. According to Lloyd, the advent of the Learning Center and Tutorial Program in 1967 directly impacted the community, as it "provided an opportunity for the less advantaged and less well-prepared students to attain the requisite standards for full admission into the College's various

Chartered in 1963, the Columbus College Foundation acquires funds in support of the educational activities of Columbus College. A dedicated board of trustees helps fulfill this mission. Pictured, left to right, are board members Pete Morrow, MacAllister Isaacs, Jim Byars, and Howell Hollis.

degree programs." (Lloyd, *Their Time*, p.7) Annual funding for the foundation increased rapidly, and by 1976, director of development Roy Tanner reported that between 1965 and 1976, the Foundation provided approximately $1.5 million in support of a variety of programs at the college, many of which would not have been possible if the college relied only on state funding.

Jack Passailaique, left, was one of the original members of the Columbus College Foundation. Jim Byars, right, served as the first treasurer of the Columbus College Foundation Executive Committee.

The expansion of the college during the 1960s and 1970s coincided with a period of social unrest in the United States that left its mark on both the students and the campuses they attended. As was customary in the South, when it was founded in 1958, Columbus College was a segregated institution, with attendance limited to white students. In 1958, however, the civil rights movement was gaining momentum, in part because of the Brown *v.* Board of Education ruling handed down by the United

States Supreme Court in 1954. This ruling declared segregation to be illegal in public schools and ordered schools to begin the process of desegregation with "all deliberate speed." Although originally intended to address public schools, in effect the Supreme Court's ruling overturned segregation itself and eventually led to integration in a wide range of social spaces, including colleges.

By the early 1960s, the Board of Regents of the University System of Georgia was forced to confront integration head

John Townsend, the first African American student to attend Columbus College, enrolled in 1963 and received his associate's degree in 1965. Townsend is shown here with the 1964–1965 Student Government Association, in which he served as a representative.

on, when Charlayne Hunter and Hamilton Holmes filed suit against the University of Georgia for denying them admission based on race. A court order permitted Hunter and Holmes to register in January 1961, and violent protests broke out as the two threatened not only the legal barriers that separated white from black in the Jim Crow South, but social barriers as well.

Integration would come much more peacefully to Columbus College. In the summer of 1963, John Townsend, an African American graduate of Spencer High School, applied for admission to the college. Whitley had no doubts about Townsend's qualifications to complete college-level work, and in a 1982 oral history interview, Whitley stated that he called the Board of Regents office to "tell them we did have an applicant who, if he were white, there'd be no question about his enrollment." Both Whitley and other school officials realized it was not a matter of *if* the integration of Columbus College would occur, it was a matter of when, and Townsend represented the when by applying for fall 1963 admission. Townsend enrolled with little fanfare, and unlike the University of Georgia, there were no violent protests.

The fact that there were no major protests did not mean that the Columbus College students actively supported integration. Asked in 2007 about whether students accepted Townsend at the time, faculty member Lindsey Mock responded by stating that "...accepting, you have to be careful when you use that word, because you interpret silence as acceptance and that may not be true. Because some people may be quiet but you never know what they may be thinking in their hearts and minds about it." At least one major incident occurred in which Townsend's locker was set on fire, an indication that not all members of the college community welcomed its first African American student. Still, Townsend persisted, engaging in extracurricular activities as a member of the Student Government Association and working with the college literary magazine, *Spectrum*. He received his

associate's degree in June 1965 and then continued his studies at the University of Georgia, eventually earning a bachelor's degree in political science, a master's in adult education, and a doctorate in education psychology and educational administration. Through his perseverance and dedication, John Townsend admirably and honorably paved the way for an increasing number of African American students at the college. In a November 12, 1964, interview published in the college newspaper, Townsend summed up his attitude toward Columbus College: "I am glad I have had the chance to attend Columbus College; I take pride in knowing that other Negroes may follow me now and the education that they receive will help them, as it has helped me."

Columbus College integrated in 1963. John Townsend is pictured here with the staff of *Spectrum*, the literary magazine of the college. Other members of the staff include Cliff Britton, Mike Agnew, Sterling Eisiminger, and Wayne Mergler.

As an integrated facility, Columbus College truly became an institution of higher learning open to the entire community, since at least a third of the population of the surrounding region was African American. As more African Americans signed up for classes and came to identify with the institution, other civil rights issues came to the forefront. In particular, students of color found the Rebel mascot and the playing of "Dixie" at sporting events to be especially demeaning. While

The Cosmopolitan Club, later renamed the Black Student Union, advocated equal rights and championed diversity on the Columbus College campus. The group first organized in the fall of 1968.

students both black and white attempted to remove the mascot democratically, a core group of students resisted this change in school tradition. Heated exchanges took place between students who supported the Rebel and those who felt the time was ripe for elimination of the controversial symbol.

Some change did occur, however, as in April 1969 the student body voted to replace the original school colors of gold and grey with the more patriotic red, white, and blue, and in January 1970 the Student Government Association agreed to ban the playing of "Dixie" at basketball games. After nearly three years of futile attempts to remove the mascot and the failure of a student referendum on the subject, the administration took up the matter, and on February 27, 1970, President Thomas Y. Whitley announced that the Rebel would no longer serve as the college mascot. Reflecting on the matter after his retirement,

The 1970–1971 officers of the Black Student Union were, left to right, president Robert Dixon, secretary-treasurer Peggy Ruggs, and vice president Ricky Florence. The group sponsored the second Black Day at Columbus College on May 21, 1971.

# Rebel Spirit

## COLUMBUS COLLEGE
### Columbus, Georgia

The Rebel served as the college mascot from 1958–1970. This Rebel logo appeared on the cover of the first Student Handbook, published in 1965–1966.

Whitley wished the scenario had played out differently but realized that "a majority of the faculty might have been willing to go along with the changing of the name of the mascot, but I'm not sure that a majority of the students would not have favored it or did not favor it." (Whitley, p.41) Although the removal of the mascot was in the best interest of the college and community,

# CC President Removes Rebel Mascot

*Faculty Division Heads Support Move*

President Thomas Y. Whitley announced on February 27 that the Rebel mascot will no longer be a part of Columbus College as of or before the official end of this school year.

The announcement was made at a special called assembly of the student body and faculty members, held in the Fine Arts Hall auditorium. Dr. Charles A. Parker, Chairman of the Education Division, and Lon Marlowe, President of the Student Government Association, also spoke at the assembly.

Dr. Whitley stated that "this is the third year we have had lengthy discussions on the mascot." He said he had hoped that as the number of black students at Columbus College increased, the student body itself would make the change. "This assembly," he added, "is the culmination of the problem of this year."

Dr. Parker gave the contents of a recommendation made by the division chairmen after a meeting held approximately three weeks and before the assembly, and the reasons for the recommendation. He stated that as the diversity of the student body here is increasing and will continue to increase, the controversy over the mascot would continue unless a change were made.

**Disruptive Factor**

This controversy, he said, has become a disruptive factor on campus, since the present mascot and symbol have not provided unity as they should do. Therefore, the division chairmen recommended unanimously that Dr. Whitley remove the Rebel from contention as the mascot. This recommendation was accepted by Dr. Whitley.

Lon Marlowe then described the

A brochure containing illustrations and explanations of the symbolism involved in each was distributed at the beginning of the assembly. Mr. Marlowe announced that anyone wishing to submit another choice for mascot must bring it, along with a suitable illustration and a petition bearing the names of 200 Columbus College students, to the March 4 meeting of SGA. In the March 10 and 11 elections to determine the new mascot, however, the three original alternatives will still be on the ballot, and whichever of those receives the highest number of votes will be given the cash prize, regardless of whether or not it becomes the new mascot.

Dr. Whitley also stated that he wished to recognize Andrew Henderson, Ray Lakes, and Jackie Marsha. These students, he said, met with him and assured him that the basketball team would support the basketball team at home games. He added that there had been a great improvement in school spirit since that time, and that he especially wished to thank Mr. Lakes for his leadership in the matter.

In response to a student who asked, "By whose authority is the Rebel removed as mascot?" Dr. Whitley answered, "I take full responsibility, and I do have the authority." After several more questions, the assembly was dismissed.

Columbus College President Thomas Y. Whitley spoke at the Mascot Assembly and announced that the Rebel will no longer be CC's mascot.

| FEE PAYMENT | |
| --- | --- |
| MARCH 17 | |
| BUSINESS OFFICE | |

# The Saber

Vol. XII—No. 11    COLUMBUS COLLEGE, COLUMBUS, GEORGIA 31907    March 13, 1970

REACTION TO MASCOT ASSEMBLY . . .
Letters, Page 3.

## SGA Recommends Administrative

In February 1970, Dr. T. Y. Whitley banned the use of the Rebel as the college mascot.

Whitley's action evoked strong feelings on both sides of the issue. The wounds slowly began to heal two months later, as in a runoff election to determine a new moniker, the Cougars defeated the Titans and became the new mascot of Columbus College.

This action was not a magic solution to all of the issues facing African American students on campus, however, and a variety of groups and individuals worked to promote African American culture on campus. In 1968, the Cosmopolitan Club, later known as the Black Student Union, formed to "stimulate the study of contemporary culture, emphasize the importance of achieving excellence, and encourage participation in campus activities." (*Sentry*, 1969, p.141) They also sponsored Black Day on the college campus, and the 1971 celebration featured a jam session, a black fashion show, a dance, and a soul food eat out. In 1975, black students called for non-criminal, non-violent protests if the administration failed to recognize racial discrimination on campus. They pointed out that only fourteen percent of the college population was African American, compared to thirty percent of Muscogee County, and that out of 175 faculty members, only

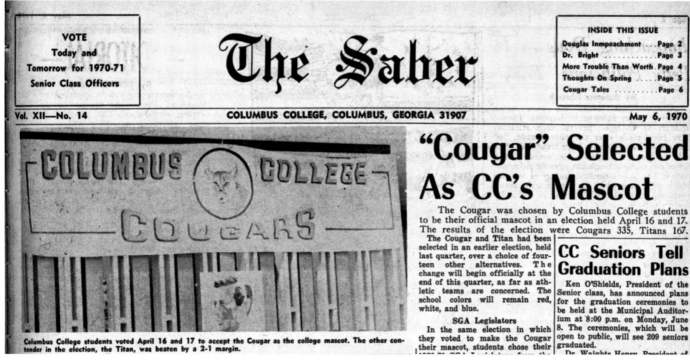

# The Saber

INSIDE THIS ISSUE

Douglas Immpeachment .... Page 2
Dr. Bright ........... Page 3
More Trouble Than Worth .Page 4
Thoughts On Spring .... Page 5
Cougar Tales ......... Page 6

Vol. XII—No. 14     COLUMBUS COLLEGE, COLUMBUS, GEORGIA 31907     May 6, 1970

## "Cougar" Selected As CC's Mascot

The Cougar was chosen by Columbus College students to be their official mascot in an election held April 16 and 17. The results of the election were Cougars 335, Titans 167.

The Cougar and Titan had been selected in an earlier election, held last quarter, over a choice of fourteen other alternatives. The change will begin officially at the end of this quarter, as far as athletic teams are concerned. The school colors will remain red, white, and blue.

### SGA Legislators

In the same election in which they voted to make the Cougar their mascot, students chose their

### CC Seniors Tell Graduation Plans

Ken O'Shields, President of the Senior class, has announced plans for the graduation ceremonies to be held at the Municipal Auditorium at 8:00 p.m. on Monday, June 8. The ceremonies, which will be open to public, will see 209 seniors graduated.

Dr. Weights Henry, President of

Columbus College students voted April 16 and 17 to accept the Cougar as the college mascot. The other contender in the election, the Titan, was beaten by a 2-1 margin.

In April 1970, students voted in a new mascot to replace the Rebel, the Cougar. The school also selected new colors, replacing grey and gold with red, white, and blue.

two were African American. A meeting between administration and African American students defused the situation, although the meeting did not result in the immediate change sought by the students. This incident shined light on the fact that despite a decade of progress in the area of racial equality, Columbus College still had large strides to make to be truly representative of the community as a whole. The actions also proved that although the college might be conservative, the students and faculty could affect cultural change when they believed strongly that it was warranted.

One of the first African American students to play basketball for Columbus College was Gary Dozier, a member of the 1968–1969 team. This was also the first year the school competed on the senior college level.

Although labeled as a conservative campus, members of the campus community also participated in other social protest movements such as the Vietnam War and the "streaking" fad. The conservative nature of the student body was reflected in a campus poll conducted in 1969, which found that a majority of students on campus supported the war effort. This result, although uncommon for a college campus at the time, was a predictable outcome for a college composed mainly of local commuter students, many who had either family or friends in military service. A number of faculty and students did engage in anti-war protests; however, they did not turn violent like the incident at Kent State University in May 1970, when four students were shot to death by National Guard troops as they protested the United States' invasion of Cambodia.

A much more lighthearted and often-remembered social protest movement at Columbus College was the "streaker week" of March 6th through 8th, 1974, when a number of college students ran nude through the campus. Possibly in response to Ray Stevens' smash hit "They Call Him the Streak," college campuses across the nation became the scene of naked men and women racing across campus. At a fellow Board of Regents institution, the University of Georgia, a reported record for simultaneous streaking occurred on March 7, 1974, with some 1,549 participants. Although on other campuses such events often took place at night, at Columbus College streaking took place during the day, and students would began their bare journey in the Davidson Center and run across the heart of campus to Howard Hall in front of crowds estimated as large as four hundred people. The approach of the campus administration was to allow those participating to exercise their right to rebel, as cracking down on the behavior might lead to greater and more prolonged instances of streaking. When asked about his opinion of the event by a local reporter, President T. Y. Whitley responded "I think I am a little bit too old to streak. It's a fad just like swallowing goldfish was. The sap rises in the spring

and so do the saps. You tend to have some erratic behavior." While the campus community appeared amused by the behavior, many community members were outraged that such shenanigans went unpunished on the college campus. In an interview published in the Columbus College *Saber* dated October 10, 1974, Columbus Chief of Police Curtis McClung offered his take on the situation: "Just because we've let streaking slide doesn't mean we are going to turn Columbus College into a nudist colony. Because of the carnival-like atmosphere created at Columbus College by the streakers, it was officially looked upon as a fad as long as it was confined to campus. By law we can interfere with a misdemeanor on campus, but this is not a practice. Had the police gone out and arrested those students participating in the streaking, we would have alienated five hundred to a thousand students against the police. I conferred with Dr. Whitley and decided streaking should be considered a school activity—it was their problem. We stood ready to assist if asked."

Posted at the edge of campus, local police officers received orders to arrest any individuals violating the city decency laws, but only if the incident occurred off of the college campus. In only one instance, however, did the naked students wander off campus, at

On March 6, 1974, Columbus College students gathered to catch a glimpse of streakers racing across campus.

Dr. Thomas Y. Whitley officially retired on June 30, 1979, after twenty-one years of service to Columbus College.

One of Whitley's last official duties was to dedicate the Alumni Gateway, located at the Lindsay Creek Drive entrance to campus.

At the annual alumni meeting on June 28, 1979, outgoing alumni president Charles Eason and incoming alumni president Don Harbuck present Dr. T. Y. Whitley with a commemorative clock in appreciation of his many years of service. Mary Jo Whitley is on the left.

which time they piled into a pickup truck, only to be fully clothed when officers finally pulled them over. After three days, the novelty of streaking wore off, but not without a last minute appearance by Lady Godiva, horse and all! In a *Saber* article dated October 10, 1974, one Columbus college student offered an alternative opinion on the activity: "Streaking does not fit into the college campus. It affects the faith of some, imposes on students, and disrupts classes." Whether serious or lighthearted, Columbus College students nonetheless proved themselves to be products of their time, influenced by cultural movements that also swept other college campuses around the nation.

By the late 1970s, the expansion that began with the moving of the campus to the former Miller Dairy site in 1963 had all but run its course. During this time, the college remained under the able leadership of Dr. T. Y Whitley and Dean John Anderson, who arrived at Columbus College in 1963. After twenty-one years as the only president the college had ever known, on Monday, February 5, 1979, Dr. T. Y. Whitley announced his intention to retire on June 30 of the same year. A leader by example, Whitley saw the campus expand from an abandoned textile mill with thirteen faculty and less than three hundred students into a regional college offering associate, bachelor's and master's degrees to a student population of more than five thousand, with courses taught by more than two hundred full-time faculty members. Dr. Lindsey Mock, who worked with Whitley for nearly two decades, remembered his former boss as "…old school, but a man with the highest integrity of any man I have ever seen."

While guiding the college though its adolescence, Whitley also found time to chair the Muscogee County Charter Commission,

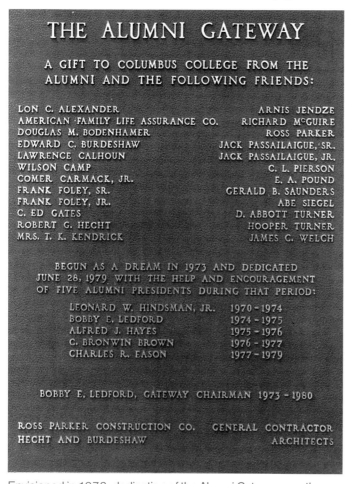

Envisioned in 1973, dedication of the Alumni Gateway was the culmination of the efforts of a number of alumni and friends of the university.

The Algonquin Drive entrance to Columbus College as it appeared in 1966

Student activities such as this banana split eating contest brought students together on the Columbus College campus.

Not only did Columbus College receive support from the community, but the faculty and students worked to contribute to the community as well. Columbus Mayor J. R. Allen signed a proclamation declaring April 18–25, 1971, as Earth Week in Columbus. Pictured are, left to right, Dr. George Stanton, Ralph Evers, Arthur Pickens, and Mayor Allen.

the result of which was the first city-county consolidated government in Georgia. Whitley served terms as director of the Columbus Chamber of Commerce, as well as president of the Georgia Association of Junior Colleges, president of the Georgia Association of Colleges, and director of the Southern Association of Junior Colleges. In recognition of his two decades of service to the region, in January 1979 the Columbus Chamber of Commerce awarded Whitley the James W. Woodruff, Jr. Memorial Award for Distinguished Citizenship.

One of Whitley's last official functions was the dedication of the Alumni Gateway on East Lindsay Creek Drive, an appropriate action, as upon his retirement on June 30, 1979, all of the alumni to whom the entrance was dedicated arrived, studied, and matriculated under his leadership and guidance. As a new decade dawned, the college was actively seeking a new leader to build on the foundation created by its first president.

The pool, located in the annex to the gymnasium, provided students with aquatic opportunities.

Another type of pool captivates this group of Columbus College students, seen here engaging in an ever-popular pastime in the Davidson Student Center.

For Homecoming 1969, student groups participated in a bed race, where competing teams modified furniture for speed.

Although popular with students, the likelihood of injury led to the demise of the activity of bed racing.

The Columbus College women's volleyball team challenges Berry College in this photograph from the 1970s.

The IPTAY-ettes supported college athletics by raising funds in support of college athletic programs. The acronym IPTAY stands for "I pay ten a year."

The 1970s also saw the expansion of fraternities and sororities to the Columbus College campus. Here, the local chapter of Tau Kappa Epsilon participates in the Columbus Bicentennial Fourth of July parade in 1976.

Student government played an important role in campus life, although at times participation was lackluster at best. Mike Blackwell bucks this trend with an innovative campaign sign in 1971.

Student political organizations formed quite early on the Columbus College campus. Here, Young Republicans president Lucius Morton chats with Bo Callaway, the 1966 Republican candidate for governor of Georgia.

The Young Democrats were the rivals of the Young Republicans. Here, John Hawkins, Jimmy Welsh, and Toni Thompson share ideas with Jimmy Carter, then a state senator. Carter would go on to serve as governor of Georgia from 1971–1975 and president of the United States from 1977–1981.

Named Miss Sentry and homecoming queen in 1968 and Miss Columbus College in 1969, Nancy Carr also acquired the title of Miss Georgia in 1970.

Ray Lakes was an active member of the Student Government Association, the Cosmopolitan Club, and the Young Democrats during his undergraduate career at Columbus College in the early 1970s.

Lon Marlowe presided over the Student Government Association as it undertook the task of selecting a new Columbus College mascot.

Editor Geri Paul watches over the *Saber* staff during her term at the helm of the student newspaper. Her many undergraduate activities included contributions to the college annual, the *Sentry*, serving as senior class treasurer, and receiving academic awards as the top American history student in 1968 and 1971. She reigned as Miss Sentry in 1970 and was awarded the Faculty Cup in 1971.

Tom Loughman poses for the camera in this 1971 image. Loughman was a member of the debate team, Choral Readers, and Lambda Iota Tau. He also took part in a number of Columbus College theatrical performances, including *Taming of the Shrew*.

## Chapter Three   New Leadership, New Challenges

*"A twenty-five-year-old college is still a very young college. An enormous amount has been accomplished at Columbus College this last quarter-century, and we can all justly be proud. . . . But of course, much yet remains to be done. I call it the 'maturing' of the college. To me that is the great challenge and the great delight of Columbus College."*

*Dr. Francis J. Brooke, Columbus College President, interview by the Columbus Magazine, May/June 1983.*

The headline of the Wednesday, May 6, 1981, Columbus College *Saber* summed up the previous year with one simple phrase: "Columbus College: The Home of the Search Committee." Reportedly, this slogan came from a faculty member, perhaps one tapped to serve on one of the numerous high-profile search committees convened during the 1980–1981 academic year. After nearly two decades of stability, the years 1980 and 1981 saw changes in the college's president, vice president for academic affairs, and vice president for business and finance, as well as the selection of a new head basketball coach. At any institution, replacing one long-term, highly visible leader is a time of uncertainty and change, but when a maturing institution is asked to replace a number of such positions, a significant challenge arises. Just such a situation faced Columbus College, as within a year president T. Y. Whitley, vice president for academic affairs John Anderson, and vice president for business and finance Jim Sanders

Taking office in August of 1980, Dr. Francis J. Brooke served as the president of Columbus College until December 31, 1987. (Photograph courtesy of the *Columbus Ledger-Enquirer*)

all left the university for either retirement or other positions. While not leaving the university, longtime head basketball coach Sonny Clements decided it was time to concentrate full time on his duties as athletic director, leaving a vacancy for one of the most visible coaching positions on campus. As the university looked

Effective January 1, 1980, Dr. William C. LeNoir became acting president of Columbus College until the Board of Regents approved a new leader of the institution.

toward its twenty-fifth anniversary in 1983, it also looked for a new generation of leaders.

The first and foremost priority of the campus was selecting a successor to Dr. T. Y. Whitley, the president of the college. Recognizing Whitley's many contributions to the school, the community rightfully sought a successor to build on this legacy and move the college forward. After the announcement of his retirement in February, a twenty-seven-member search committee formed, chaired by Dr. George Stanton, professor of biology. More than one hundred applications had arrived by July 1979, but the hiring process was just getting underway. Dr. John E. Anderson, vice president for academic affairs, stepped in to serve as acting president after Whitley's official retirement on June 30, 1979. A possible contender for elevation to president of the college, Anderson instead announced in July 1979 that he too would be leaving the college, moving on to accept the job of president at Christopher Newport College in Newport News, Virginia, effective January 1, 1980. Like Whitley, Anderson left Columbus College after many faithful years of service, coming to Columbus College

in 1963 at the age of thirty-one to serve as dean of the college, a position later renamed vice president for academic affairs. Although hopeful that the position could be filled by Anderson's departure on December 31, 1979, the careful selection of a new leader was necessarily a methodical one. With the search still in progress as fall turned to winter, the college named Dr. William LeNoir acting president, effective January 1, 1980. LeNoir would serve in this capacity until the selection of a new president.

Dr. John E. Anderson served as academic dean and vice president for academic affairs for sixteen years before accepting the position of president at Christopher Newport College in Newport News, Virginia, effective January 1, 1979.

Professor of Biology George Stanton served as the chair of the presidential search committee in 1979–1980. In 2006, he would join the administration as vice president for academic affairs.

During February, March, and April of 1980, six candidates visited campus and interviewed for the college's highest post. They included Dr. Richard P. Soter, provost at Wilkes College; Dr. Billy J. Franklin, vice president for academic affairs at Stephen F. Austin State University; Dr. Richard E. McDowell, president of the University of Pittsburgh at Bradford; Dr. Norman Parmer, former associate dean of arts and sciences at Ohio State University; Dr. Francis J. Brooke, provost at Virginia Commonwealth University; and Dr. W. Slater Hollis, vice president at the Richard Manufacturing Company and former graduate director at Hardin-Simmons University. Rumors swirled as to who the next president would be, and unsubstantiated rumors listed Brooke, Parmer, and McDowell as the top candidates.

After nearly a year without a permanent leader, on June 12, 1980, the Board of Regents of the University System of Georgia named Dr. Francis J. Brooke as president of Columbus College, effective August 1, 1980. Chairman of the search committee Stanton expressed relief at the decision, stating in a June 12, 1980, *Columbus Ledger* article that "the college is really ready for a new president," and quipping that "the mood of the school's faculty and students is one of the best ever, or at least since the streakers." With a long and difficult search over, an excited campus looked forward to settling in with its new chief executive.

As the former provost at Virginia Commonwealth University in Richmond, Virginia, Brooke had an impressive résumé. A native Virginian, he earned his doctoral degree in German from the University of North Carolina—Chapel Hill, taught at both Centre

College in Kentucky and Cornell University, and then served as the acting chairman of the Modern Language Department at the University of Virginia before rising to the position of provost at Virginia Commonwealth. At fifty-one, Brooke possessed both the teaching and administrative skills to lead the college successfully. He admitted, though, that there was no one solution to becoming familiar with members of the campus community, stating that he would likely introduce himself by "stop(ping) them and saying 'Hi, I am Frank Brooke.'" Brooke officially took office in August of 1980.

Besides greeting the new campus community, Brooke needed to replace two crucial campus administrative positions, that of vice president for academic affairs and vice president for business and finance. By May 1981, the "Year of the Search Committee" waned with the selection of Dr. Sue A. Dezendolet as vice president for academic affairs and Dr. Frank Douglas Brown as vice president for business and finance.

The hiring of Dezendolet in the summer of 1981 was a milestone for the college—the first female vice president on the campus. Dezendolet was a veteran of higher education, and her previous posts included administrative positions as the acting dean

The Columbus College leadership group during the Brooke administration included, from left to right, Dr. Lindsey Mock, Mr. Dale Crail, Dr. Lon Marlowe, Dr. Francis Brooke, Dr. Sue Dezendolet, and Dr. Frank Brown.

of academic programs at Southern Illinois at Carbondale, the associate dean of academic affairs and research at Southern Illinois University in Carbondale, and vice president for academic affairs at Sangamon State University. Dr. Dezendolet would play a key role in the Brooke administration by serving as the chief academic officer of the institution.

Dr. Frank Douglas Brown joined the leadership group in the summer of 1981 as well. As the new vice president for business and finance, Brown promised in an article in the *Saber* to "give a dollar's worth of service for every dollar [students] pay." With a doctoral degree from Florida State University in higher education

administration, Brown had worked with the IBM Corporation, the Alabama Commission of Higher Education, and just before coming to Columbus College, served as assistant chancellor for finance and operations at the University of Houston. Once at Columbus College, he immediately went to work to ensure that the university managed its funds wisely, and in his first interview with the Columbus College *Saber* in July 1, 1981, promised to place "students first and faculty second."

Although he was not a part of the administrative staff, the hiring of Coach Herbert Greene as head basketball coach in the spring of 1981 also represented another changing of the

Coach Frank "Sonny" Clements arrived at Columbus College in 1959 and retired in 1983. He built a solid athletic program and directed the college sports teams as they moved from junior college to college status in the late 1960s.

Herbert Greene became the Cougar basketball coach in 1981 and assumed the additional position of athletic director in 1983. He still guides the athletic department as director today but retired from coaching in 2006.

guard for the college. Before retiring from his position as head basketball coach at the end of the 1979–1980 season, Frank "Sonny" Clements led all but one of the prior Columbus College basketball teams, and amassed a 287-258 record as the coach of the Rebels and Cougars. His teams won two Georgia Junior College Conference titles in 1963–1964 and 1964–1965, and a South Atlantic Conference title in 1977–1978. The 1980–1981 Cougars played under interim coach David Noles, who also applied for the permanent job. Instead, a search committee selected Herbert Greene, a Eufaula native and Auburn University assistant coach, to lead the Cougars. Clements would stay on as athletic director for two more years, at which time Greene took over the athletic director's job as well. Greene would remain at the helm of the college basketball program for more than two decades.

The newly hired leaders faced a number of difficult challenges. First, enrollment at the college was in a decline that began in 1976 and would last until 1987. Although enrollment numbered 5,674 in 1975, that number dipped to 3,602 by 1987 as fewer students selected Columbus College. The period of remarkable growth the institution saw in the two prior decades was gone, and in its place was the bleak prospect of a continued descent in student numbers. Second, a series of lean budget years left the college in a situation of constantly cutting corners to meet projected shortfalls.

The combination of declining enrollment and budget cuts had a direct impact on student affairs, and by 1983 an impromptu sampling of Columbus College students rated the quality of student life as "inadequate." A November 5, 1980 visit from the chancellor of the Board of Regents of the University System of Georgia reflected the new outlook, as Chancellor Crawford informed a gathering of Columbus College students that the chances were "remote that Columbus College will ever become a university." Crawford also took a skeptical view toward constructing campus housing, noting that changing from a commuter campus to a domestic campus could be a difficult transition. A second visit from

Crawford in March 1983 brought a similar result, as again the chancellor predicted little growth for the college in the next decade. Sadly, Crawford's short-term projections were proven correct.

To complicate matters, President Brooke got off to a rocky start with some members of the college community. In the fall of 1981, Brooke created controversy by accepting an all-expenses-paid trip to the Tenth Annual Conference of the Unity of the Sciences in Seoul, South Korea. While the conference sported an academic tone with seventy-five presentations, the sponsorship of his trip by the Unification Church led by Reverend Sun Myung Moon represented an ethical problem to a number of students and faculty members. Accused at the time of federal tax evasion charges, Moon was convicted of the charges in 1982 and spent time incarcerated in a federal prison. The Unification Church also stood accused of using brainwashing techniques to recruit and retain members. Brooke defended his decision, stating, "Attendance at the meeting does not mean that you endorse the Unification Church or its teachings." Still, the incident placed him in the uncomfortable role of defending his actions to the public, an undesirable situation for a newly minted college president.

Earlier in the year, Dr. Brooke temporarily froze a Student Government Association reserve fund of fifty thousand dollars, raising questions about whether students had the right to request funding from the surplus student activity fees. Student leadership made the matter a public one, voicing their opinions on the action in both the college newspaper, the *Saber*, and throughout the community when the *Columbus Ledger-Enquirer* ran an editorial on the issue. In July 1981, Dr. Brooke called a meeting of the Student Activities Committee to clear up the situation and clarified that the student account funds were available, but merely in a separate account. The college president stated that the misunderstanding over the reserve fund was due to a lack of communication between the students and administration and his "newness" on campus, and promised that "We certainly will communicate with you" when spending future funds from the account. Although clearly a misunderstanding, the saga dragged on for nearly nine months in the student newspaper before the issue was finally put to rest, forcing Brooke into a public dialogue that created dissension on campus.

Even changes that proved worthwhile in the long term created backlash for the college. In early 1982, vice president for academic affairs Sue Dezendolet recommended the reorganization of the academic divisions into schools, each to be headed by a dean. Under her plan, backed by Dr. Brooke, the streamlined structure would consist of four schools: Arts and Letters, Science, Education, and Business. The existing schools of Education and Business would retain their current administrative heads, but new deans would be selected for Arts and Letters and Science. Not all faculty agreed with the change, but in a February faculty meeting Dr. Brooke urged that the choice to consolidate was "to the true benefit of the college." With the plan in place, Dezendolet named Dr. Paul Vander Gheynst dean of the newly created School of Arts and Letters, and Dr. William LeNoir took the reins in the School of Science, while newly hired Dr. Joseph C. Johnson headed the School of Education. Dr. Olice Embry continued his service to the college as head of the School of Business. Final approval of the restructuring plan came from the Board of Regents in June 1982, and the conversion was complete and in place for the fall quarter. One of the major accomplishments of the Brooke presidency, the realignment into four units remains the basic structure of the institution today, with the term "school" dropped in favor of the term "college" in 1998.

Music professor Dr. Paul Vander Gheynst became dean of the School of Arts and Letters in 1982.

Other major achievements of the Brooke era included a jubilant celebration of the twenty-fifth anniversary of Columbus College, and a successful capital campaign to raise much-needed private funds for the institution. The Silver Anniversary was an important milestone in the life of the college, and in 1982 a committee headed by Dr. John Lupold began planning a series of commemorative events under the theme "Reaching for Tomorrow." Dr. Craig Lloyd, history professor and later director of the college archives, prepared a booklet titled *Columbus College: Reaching for Tomorrow*, which included a historical sketch of the college and a timeline of significant events in the school's history. Lloyd noted that since the opening in 1958, the college had produced more than eight thousand graduates and had "become a vital community and regional

Attendees of the twenty-fifth anniversary celebration enjoyed slices of this one-thousand-pound birthday cake.

educational resource."(Lloyd, *Reaching for Tomorrow*, p. 12)

The culminating event of the Silver Anniversary was an open house on the college campus, held on May 14, 1983, dubbed Founders Day. Alumni, faculty, staff, and students had the option to devour pieces of a giant birthday cake estimated to weigh one thousand pounds, participate in a 6.2-mile "Silver Streak" Road Race, listen to live music, view the Fort Benning Silver Wings Parachute Team descend on Cougar Field, watch the third game of the NCAA South Atlantic Regional Tournament, or wield a bat as students took on faculty in an afternoon softball game. The day-long festival served to reacquaint the entire community with the college and infuse them with the Columbus College spirit.

Dr. Craig Lloyd (right), Columbus College history professor and director of the college archives, penned a brief history of the university for the twenty-fifth anniversary titled *Columbus College: Reaching for Tomorrow*.

As the year of Silver Anniversary celebrations drew to a close, the college embarked on another ambitious initiative: a major capital campaign. This fundraising initiative, conceived in 1983 and implemented in 1984, set a target goal of four million dollars to fund a student scholarship endowment, endowments for faculty in business and nursing, library acquisitions, instructional equipment, and improvements and renovations for campus buildings. Officially launched in October 1984, the Campaign for Excellence was under the able leadership of campaign chairman Ray E. Crowley and co-vice chairmen Hugh Landrum, Jr. and Charles A. McClure. Just eight months later, the official tally revealed that the fundraising drive exceeded all expectations by receiving contributions in excess of six million dollars. This remarkable accomplishment once again proved that the community not only believed in the mission of Columbus College but also was willing to lend financial support to the college to ensure it achieved that mission. President Brooke elegantly summed up the campaign, saying, "The community showed it not only cared about this college…but cared enough to invest in its future." (Lloyd, *Their Time, Their Influence, Their Substance,* p.15)

Campaign for Excellence leaders Hugh Landrum, William Gill, Ray Crowley, and Charles McClure celebrate the success of the capital campaign with Dr. Francis Brooke.

A successful capital campaign in 1984–1985 raised more than six million dollars to support a variety of projects at the college.

Although some students gave campus life poor ratings, excellence in academics and campus programming continued in the 1980s. Strong music and biology departments attracted students not only from Columbus but from across the state and region as well. Education and nursing provided much-needed professionals in the local area. The graduate program in education offered an important post-baccalaureate degree for those seeking to continue their college studies, and the School of Education received accreditation in 1987 from the National Council for the Accreditation of Teacher Education. The nursing program expanded to offer a bachelor's degree, first awarding the new degree in 1986. Renamed in honor of philanthropist D. Abbott Turner in 1984, the D. Abbott Turner School of Business remained a popular choice with Columbus College students. National speakers such as Alex Haley, Edward Albee, and Ralph Abernathy lectured on the campus during the decade, and the Count Basie Orchestra entertained students and the public alike in a concert in Fine Arts Hall. In 1983, a new college tradition began with the inception of the Black Applause Banquet, a celebration of Black History Month that annually invites a noted African American speaker to campus. In 1983, Dr. John Townsend, the first African American student to enroll at Columbus College, returned to campus to deliver the inaugural address.

Building on the vision of patron of the arts Ruth Schwob, the Columbus College Music Department developed into a program of excellence. Professors Patricio Cobos, Rex Whiddon, and Marcia Riley contributed to this growth.

In addition to these academic and cultural opportunities, the college maintained its tradition of athletic prowess. In both 1978 and 1980, the Columbus College golf team under Coach Mike Taylor captured the NCAA Division II national championships, the first ever for the school. Coach Charles Ragsdale, who revived the college baseball team in 1970, quickly built the Cougars into a solid team, and by the last season of his tenure as coach, the team vied for a national championship in 1984 in the NCAA Division II College World Series. Retiring after fifteen years at the helm of the program, Ragsdale compiled a 466-269-5 record, including a 42-12-1 record in his final season.

In 1986, the baseball team would again advance to the College World Series, this time under the leadership of Coach Derek

Mann. The Cougars advanced to the championship game, where they faced regional rival Troy State, who handed the Columbus College squad a 5-0 defeat. A reloaded Cougar squad again played in the Division II College World Series in 1987 but fell in the semi-final game to the University of Tampa.

Basketball continued to field a solid program under new coach Herbert Greene, who also became athletic director upon the retirement of Frank "Sonny" Clements in 1983. The major disappointment in athletics was a proposed move from NCAA

Charles Ragsdale shaped the Cougar baseball teams into winners, compiling a 466-269-5 record in fifteen years as head coach. Ragsdale retired in 1985.

The 1986 Cougar baseball team reached the College World Series, falling to Troy State University 5-0 in the championship game.

Division II to NCAA Division I status in 1984, which was abandoned in 1985. Although a move to Division I appeared feasible in 1984, a change in NCAA rules requiring schools to field six men's and six women's athletic teams left the college short three athletic teams, and would also have required the Lady Cougar athletes to move from the less competitive NAIA to the top level of competition in NCAA. Combined with an increase in tuition that drove up the cost of athletic scholarships, athletic director Herbert Greene, in consultation with President Francis Brooke, made the decision to remain in NCAA Division II. While disappointed by the turn of events, Greene admitted in an interview published in the Columbus College *Saber* on May 1, 1985, that the move to forgo entry into Division I was in the best interest of the school and its athletes: "It's one of the toughest things I've had to do since

I've been at Columbus College. But there was no way I could lead the Athletic Department into that type of situation."

A declining state budget not only raised the price of tuition but impacted college operations as well. In 1982, budget cuts of $280,000 hit the college, followed by a downward adjustment of $167,000 in 1983. By December 1984, the college made the drastic move of releasing several faculty and staff members, including two non-tenured music professors. Eroding student enrollment also factored into the slashes in state monies, and by 1986, the institution faced the prospect of trimming the budget by a massive eight hundred thousand dollars.

Despite the success of the Campaign for Excellence in 1984–1985, these years of monetary frugality slowly eroded the morale of the Columbus College faculty, many of whom were senior, tenured members of the university system. The majority of senior faculty was fiercely loyal to Columbus College, and early in the decade looked to the administration for solutions to the crises at hand.

Unfortunately, by 1986 it was clear that most faculty members had lost faith in President Francis Brooke, and to a lesser extent, vice president for academic affairs Sue Dezendolet. Already stirring controversy on campus with the 1981 Unification Church-sponsored trip to Korea, Brooke also strengthened tenure requirements, a move that rankled some faculty members. In 1983, a $900,000 landscape plan, which enhanced the aesthetics of the campus, came under fire by both students and faculty members as a poor use of funds for a campus enduring a lean budget cycle. In a move to alleviate budget shortfalls, cuts were made in summer teaching overloads, a source of extra income for some faculty members. This reduction, while understood to be in the best interest of the institution, further eroded faculty morale.

The selection of a new dean of the business school in 1984–1985 also strained the relationship between the president and faculty, as the candidate selected for the position did not meet the approval of some of the faculty search committee members and one student member of the search committee.

Concerned about the perceived lack of leadership, in the spring of 1986 four college faculty members mailed a twenty-question anonymous survey to 147 full-time faculty members. Among the questions on the survey was a vote of confidence in the president; out of 91 respondents, 73 stated they had no confidence in Dr. Brooke's leadership. After five years of simmering, the cauldron of faculty discontent had finally reached the boiling point at Columbus College.

The survey made headlines in both the campus and local newspapers, and the local television media aired the results to the community. A copy of the survey and results also landed on Chancellor Dean Propst's desk at the Board

of Regents of the University System of Georgia. While Propst immediately scheduled a day-long visit to campus to mediate the situation, President Brooke in an April 5, 1986, interview with the *Columbus Ledger-Enquirer* stated that he had "absolutely no intention to resign" in the wake of the survey.

Dr. Virginia Spencer Carr taught at Columbus College until 1985. Carr authored two major biographies while at Columbus College: *The Lonely Hunter: A Biography of Carson McCullers* and *Dos Passos: A Life*.

Ruth Schwob remained a patron of the fine arts until her death in 1981. Here Dr. T. Y. Whitley and Jack M. Passailaique pose with a bust of Mrs. Schwob. Today the bust is located in the Music Library in the RiverCenter for the Performing Arts.

Visiting campus on April 23, 1986, Propst urged the campus to work toward a resolution. The April 30, 1986 *Saber* quoted his advice: "…some very real problems and concerns…must be addressed and he (Brooke) is willing to address them." Propst also sent a message to the college faculty, stating that the college "exists for the education of the students who place their trust in our hands." The chancellor's advice, while well founded, did not produce results. In the fall of 1986, vice president for academic affairs Sue Dezendolet resigned her position at the college. Although citing personal aspirations as the reason for her departure, the stressful campus situation likely contributed to her decision to move on to other endeavors.

Dezendolet's resignation did not bode well for Brooke, and in January 1987 a second survey of campus faculty circulated. Sensing a second vote of no confidence, on Friday, February 6, 1987, Dr. Francis Brooke announced his resignation as

Dr. T.Y. Whitley and registrar Mary Livengood chat about old times while President Francis Brooke looks on. Livengood, a member of the original Columbus College administrative staff, retired in 1987.

Dr. Olice Embry served as dean of the College of Business until 1984. He retired from Columbus State University in 2006.

A January 1982 snowstorm closed campus for two days but didn't deter a snowball fight at the Simon Schwob Memorial Library.

president of Columbus College, effective June 30, 1987. In his resignation letter, published in the February 11, 1987, Columbus College *Saber*, Brooke stated his reasons for leaving the college: "The 1980s have not been easy times for higher education in general and Columbus College in particular…to be able to respond carefully and creatively, the faculty and the president must share a sense of collegiality, comfort, and harmony with each other. In recent months it has become evident there is an atmosphere of tension surrounding my presidency which is detracting from the quality of teaching, scholarship, and service. Thus I have decided that it is in the best interest of Columbus College that I leave office, and I request that I not be reappointed to the presidency for another year."

Brooke was indeed correct; the 1980s proved to be difficult for a maturing Columbus College. The sense of optimism and the exciting possibility of new leadership that existed at the beginning of the decade slowly faded as the many challenges facing both Columbus College and higher education took their toll on the university community. As the leader of the college, Dr. Francis Brooke worked to confront these challenges, successfully reorganizing the college structure, overseeing a successful celebration of the silver anniversary, participating

Fine Arts Hall served as the home of the college theatre until 2007. This production of *Barefoot in the Park* premiered in 1986.

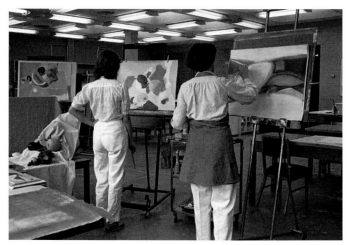

Students hone their painting skills in the art studio, then located in Fine Arts Hall. The art program has become one of the region's best.

Nursing students complete an exam in Illges Hall. The nursing program is vital to providing Columbus and the surrounding region with quality health care professionals.

Columbus College students stroll across the pedestrian bridge toward Stanley Hall and Jordan Hall.

in a highly effective Campaign for Excellence, and working to ensure that continued quality remained the standard for student academic and athletic programs. Although he was recognized for his many successes as chief executive of the college, it was ultimately a lack of faith in that same presidential leadership that caused the Columbus College family to splinter and engage in internal conflict. With the public conflict resolved, Columbus College found itself in late 1987 in the same position as it had been in 1980: the home of the search committee.

Alfonso Biggs, local African American folklorist, lectures on campus. Today, a scholarship in his honor funds history students as they seek to discover the past.

Francis Brooke and former congressman Jack Brinkley survey archival materials donated to the Columbus College Archives by Brinkley in 1982. (Photograph courtesy of the *Columbus Ledger-Enquirer*)

Merryll S. Penson served as director of the Simon Schwob Memorial Library from 1984 until 1998. She is now executive director of library services for the University System of Georgia, where she oversees projects such as GALILEO and the Digital Library of Georgia.

By 1985, Columbus College alumni numbered more than eight thousand. Evelyn Turner Pugh, a member of the Columbus City Council since 1988, received her degree from Columbus College in 1985.

## Chapter Four

To University Status and Beyond

"I believe Dr. Brown's presidency will be noted for not only its philosophical collegiality, but also for the development and implementation of a vision of what the college can be as it serves the Columbus community."

*Dr. H. Dean Propst, chancellor of the Board of Regents of the University System of Georgia, from remarks made upon the appointment of Dr. Frank D. Brown as the third president of Columbus College, January 1988*

A festive atmosphere enveloped the Columbus College campus during the third week of October 1988. Five days of celebratory events kicked off on the campus green with a jazz concert by P. J. and Company and barbecue by Country's, while events scheduled later in the week included a presentation by Dr. David Burnett King of Oregon State University entitled "Higher Education and the Crises of our Time" and a concert by the visiting pianist Panayis Lyras, accompanied by the college orchestra. Although the celebration occurred as the school began its thirtieth year, the events were not marking another milestone anniversary, but instead the inauguration of the third college president. The culminating

The inauguration of Dr. Frank D. Brown as the third president of Columbus College on October 18, 1988. The Presidential Mace, foreground, and the Presidential Medallion were first used at this ceremony.

The Thomas Y. Whitley Clock Tower.
(Photograph by Terri A. Kimble)

event in this week of pageantry was the official inauguration ceremony, which took place on Friday, October 21, 1988, in front of an overflow crowd in Fine Arts Hall. In many ways, the occasion marked a rebirth and rejuvenation of the college that would last for twenty years.

In the wake of Dr. Francis Brooke's resignation in February 1987, Chancellor Propst of the Board of Regents of the University System of Georgia appointed a search committee headed by Dr. William Frazier to select the third president for the college. On a campus recently marred by distrust between faculty and administration, the selection of a new president who possessed outstanding leadership and communication skills was vital to the future of the institution. During a comprehensive search conducted in the summer and fall of 1988, the committee narrowed the field to four final candidates: Dr. Rolanda Bonachea, acting president of Duquesne University; Dr. Frank D. Brown, vice president for business and finance at Columbus College; Dr. Thomas Hegarty, vice president for academic affairs at Butler University; and Ron Tuttle, president of the University of South Carolina—Beaufort. With Dr. Brooke leaving his post effective December 31, 1987, Dr. William LeNoir once again assumed the role of acting president of the college. This time, his tenure would be brief, as on January 14, 1988, the Board of Regents officially named Dr. Frank Douglas Brown as president of Columbus College.

The new president was not a stranger to the campus or the community. A native Alabaman with a wealth of higher education experience, Brown first arrived on campus in July 1981 as vice president for business and finance, promising to focus on efficiently and effectively administering the financial affairs of the institution. His forthright demeanor and openness while tackling difficult budget problems earned him respect from faculty, staff, and students. Taking part in the successful Campaign for Excellence, Brown also established a solid reputation with the Columbus community. Dr. H. Dean Propst identified a key quality much needed by the new leader of the college, a quality readily evident in Brown: vision. In officially announcing Brown's appointment by the Board of Regents, Propst seminally predicted that the Brown presidency would be marked by "the development and implementation of a vision of what the college can be as it serves the Columbus community."

The vision began to take shape immediately. Seeking input for a plan to move Columbus College forward, Brown wrote in the January 27, 1988, *Saber*: "I believe we have a good college, with academic programs on par with our sister institutions and in some cases a level higher…But of course we realize improvements can always be made and we are interested in moving Columbus College to the forefront of senior instructions within our state and region. Give us your ideas on ways we can accomplish this goal."

The president's staff, circa 1988. Front row, left to right, Dr. Lindsey Mock, vice president of student affairs, Dr. Frank Brown, president, Dr. William LeNoir, acting vice president for academic affairs. In the back row, left to right, Ms. Arlene Johnson, special assistant to the president, Mr. Thomas Austin, director of development, Dr. Lon Marlowe, assistant to the president, Mr. Charles Pattillo, acting vice president for business and finance, and Mr. Dale Crail, public relations director.

A campus retreat in May 1988 actively engaged the faculty in shaping the future direction of the campus, and Brown held monthly faculty sessions to promote communication between administration and faculty members. While one year earlier apathy all but paralyzed the college, by the summer of 1988 the campus was ready to move forward under new leadership. In his inaugural address, Brown outlined a path forward for the university. First, bricks from the razed Shannon Hosiery Mill would be used to "erect a monument which will serve as a reminder of our beginnings as well as a beacon for the future." Second, community partnerships between the city, the school system, and Columbus College would be emphasized, creating better educational opportunities for the good of the community. Third, Columbus College would become "a center for excellence in the arts and in the humanities." This goal included a program to strengthen "international education and international awareness." Fourth, he stated the goal of Columbus College, as a mirror of the Board of Regents of the University System of Georgia, should be to "serve our students." Brown summed up his inaugural address with the following pledges::

"We pledge a college which demands performance from its students—and offers a solid educational foundation in return;

We pledge a college that is responsive to its community and plays the full partnership role expected of it;

We pledge a college that provides a challenging program for the outstanding student as well as an opportunity to the student who has shown only marginal academic accomplishments;

And, we pledge a college of community service, dedicated to a better life, through education, for all its people. Join hands with us as we prepare for a bright, bright future."

Not merely an exercise of academic pomp and circumstance, the initiatives outlined in the inaugural speech represented

Dr. Thomas Jones served as vice president for academic affairs from 1988 until 2000, when he accepted the position of president at Armstrong Atlantic State University.

a blueprint that the institution pursued for the next twenty years as it moved from a struggling senior college with thirty-six hundred students to a thriving state university with a student enrollment of more than seventy-five hundred.

Joining Brown in implementing these goals were two new vice presidents. The college hired Dr. Thomas Z. Jones as vice president for academic affairs, effective in the fall quarter of 1988. Prior to his appointment at Columbus College, Jones served in a variety of capacities at the West Virginia Institute of Technology, including

became permanent, and he took on a post that he would hold for nearly twenty years. With his leadership team in place, on January 19, 1990, Brown outlined a new, lofty goal: to attain university status by 1993.

The new science building, renamed in honor of Professor William LeNoir in 1997, opened in 1990.

Charles Pattillo served as vice president for business and finance from 1989 until his retirement in 2006.

vice president for academic affairs. The new vice president for business and finance was an internal promotion: Charles Pattillo. A 1970 Columbus College graduate, Pattillo returned to the school in 1984, serving as a comptroller and budget director before being named the acting vice president for business and finance in February 1988. One-and-a-half years later, his appointment

Columbus College acquired the Courtyard on College in 1990 to serve student housing needs. Today, apartments on the main campus and downtown house twelve hundred students.

To attain this ambitious goal, campus facilities needed many upgrades, and renewal and rebirth became a theme on the campus. A newly refurbished Howard Hall greeted students in the fall of 1988. More importantly, groundbreaking for a new science building, the first new construction on the campus since the completion of Jordan Hall in 1977, promised much-needed classroom and laboratory space. In 1990, the college took a positive step toward providing student housing when it acquired the Courtyard on College Drive for utilization as a college dormitory.

Possibly the most important addition to the campus was a symbolic one: the Thomas Y. Whitley Clock Tower. In 1988, the Muscogee School District announced plans to demolish the Shannon Hosiery Mill, the first home of Columbus College, in order to build a new elementary school. The Columbus College

Faculty and staff clean bricks to be used in the construction of the Thomas Y. Whitley Clock Tower.

The Thomas Y. Whitley Clock Tower under construction, 1991.

Alumni Association recast nostalgia into a living monument with a plan to salvage bricks from the old mill to create a new symbol for the university. As the old mill crumbled in early 1989, crews transported bricks to the Columbus College campus, where they were cleaned and readied for reapplication as a new clock tower. Rising seventy feet above the campus green, the vertical brick structure evoked reflective memories of the tower at the original Shannon Mill site.

As the firm of Neal, Kendust & Murray drafted the designs for the clock tower, former Columbus College alumni president Wallace Kite began raising funds for the structure. At the groundbreaking for the edifice on November 28, 1990, Kite related the impact of the monument on campus, stating in an interview in the Columbus College *Saber*: "The clock tower has already become a signature for the college. It's being used on stationery, alumni parking decals, and tee shirts—when the actual construction is completed, I think we will see some very positive things start to happen. The clock tower will be recognized by students, faculty, staff, alumni, and the community as a symbol of Columbus College—where we originated, how far we have come, and how bright our future is."

Kite's evaluation was indeed correct: the Thomas Y. Whitley Clock Tower became the symbol of Columbus College even before its completion and dedication on September 20, 1991. On hand for the ceremony was Dr. Whitley, to whom the new structure paid tribute. Looking to the future, community members and faculty also placed a time capsule at the foot of the structure, to be opened on May 14, 2058, the hundredth anniversary of the college. As the crowd gazed at the clock tower silhouetted against the autumn sky, the chimes rang out, bringing to life the new face of the college.

The newly built tower soars over outdoor graduation exercises, 1991.

Groundbreaking for the Coca-Cola Space Science Center, which opened in 1996 in uptown Columbus.

Another key initiative of the new administration was a renewed collaboration with the local community to enhance learning. Such joint projects impacted the spectrum of education, from kindergarten through graduate level work, and expanded learning opportunities for the residents of the region. In 1989, the Columbus Regional Mathematics Collaborative opened at the college with the goal of establishing a resource center for teachers and students. The Mathematics Collaborative joined the Center for Excellence in Science and Education, a joint venture between the School of Science and the School of Education begun in 1993. The Center for Excellence in Science and Education soon provided oversight for two new facilities: Oxbow Meadows Environmental Learning Center and the Coca-Cola Space Science Center, which opened in 1995 and 1996, respectively.

The Oxbow Meadows Environmental Learning Center is a joint effort between the college, the municipal government, and Columbus Water Works. Located on a former landfill site, the center educates visitors about the environment of the

Oxbow Meadows Environmental Learning Center opened in 1995. It is a cooperative effort with the Columbus Water Works and is also supported by the Muscogee County School District.

In celebration of the facility's tenth anniversary, the Treetop Trail opened at Oxbow Meadows in 2005.

Chattahoochee Valley and in particular its watershed. By 2001, the facility hosted more than eighteen thousand visitors annually.

The Coca-Cola Space Science Center is a multi-purpose venue containing a Challenger Learning Center, a planetarium, and an observatory. In the first five years of operation, the center received more than three hundred thousand visits, making it one of the most popular educational destinations in the Chattahoochee Valley. These venues provide experience beyond the classroom for a variety of learners, from preschoolers to adults, and serve as a stellar example of the impact joint college and community projects can have on Columbus and the surrounding region.

Columbus College also engaged in innovative projects with area businesses. In October 1990, the college teamed with Total Systems Services, Inc. (TSYS) and Columbus Technical College in a curriculum to train employees as computer programmers. Each student enrolled in the program received credits toward an associate's or bachelor's degree in computer science. Forty-nine students entered the program in 1990, and the success of this first class encouraged future growth. In February 1992, Columbus College and TSYS announced a six-million-dollar plan to expand the training program. In conjunction with this effort, the college also secured a $2.5-million grant from IBM designated for seven

Vice President of the United States Albert Gore, Jr. visited Columbus in March 1998 to see firsthand the results of the ICAPP/COMPASS venture.

The computer science department developed into one of the best programs in the state during the 1990s.

campus computer labs, each with twenty-eight seats, software programs, and related services. Named COMPASS: Charting a New Course for Business and Education, the cooperative venture also added a new degree program at the college: applied computer science. The first students graduated in August 1993.

The endeavor expanded further still in 1996, when TSYS announced plans to build a hundred-million-dollar corporate campus and headquarters in downtown Columbus. This expansion would eventually place twenty-five hundred students in training programs at the college, supported in part by a twenty-three-million-dollar state funded Intellectual Capital Partnership Program (ICAPP) grant. The grant was a key part of an effort to keep TSYS's corporate headquarters in its hometown of Columbus.

The effort gained national recognition in March 1998 when Vice President of the United States Al Gore, Jr. traveled to Columbus to see the innovative program firsthand, which he then

United States Senator Max Cleland visits the ICAPP/COMPASS instruction lab in Stanley Hall.

highlighted in his 1999 conference "21$^{st}$ Century Skills for 21$^{st}$ Century Jobs." During his visit, Gore said that "We are in a new and different age, the information age, and the strategic resource of the information age is knowledge."

In 1999, a second ICAPP initiative with Aflac commenced, with the goal of training two hundred technology professionals for the Columbus-based insurance company. The success of the programs is lauded as a model for workforce training and is a prime example of the close ties between the college and the local business community. As a result of the impact of this program on the curriculum, the institution renamed the computer science department in honor of TSYS in 2003.

The college also began to widen opportunities in international education and to increase efforts to promote international awareness. As outlined in President Brown's inaugural address, developing and sustaining a program of excellence in this area would be a main component of the long-range plan of the college. In the early 1990s, three grants from the United States Department of Education helped move the institution closer to this goal. The first, a sixty-thousand-dollar Fulbright Hays Faculty Development Grant from the United States Department of Education, allowed faculty members the opportunity to develop skills in global education by visiting Africa. The second grant from the United States Information Agency enabled a three-year faculty exchange program with India's Madras Christian College.

The most important of the three grants was a $225,000 United States Department of Education Grant to create programming for the college and eight other Board of Regents of the University System of Georgia schools in the southwestern region of the state. The three-year grant established a program based at Columbus College to enrich international education in the region for both students and faculty members. With a growing emphasis on international education, the college formed the Center for International Education in the fall of 1995 to coordinate the wide variety of international education initiatives. In 1998, Dr. Neal McCrillis took over the program, serving as Mildred Miller Fort Foundation Distinguished Chair of International Education and director of the Center for International Education.

The Center for International Education is a statewide leader in all aspects of international education, oversees study abroad programs for students, coordinates international faculty development programs, and serves as a resource for visiting international students. The center also administers two programs to bring visiting scholars to campus, the Elena Diaz-Verson Amos Eminent Scholar in Latin American Studies and the Mildred Miller Fort Visiting Scholar in European Studies. Each scholar

The Kiryu Garden, located adjacent to Richards Hall, is sponsored by participants in the English Language Institute.

visits for a semester, teaching courses at the college and sharing their knowledge with the local community through presentations. In addition to its home in the International House on the main campus, the Center for International Education also administers a year-round study abroad program based at the Spencer House in Oxford, England. A generous gift in 2003 from the J. Kyle and Sara D. Spencer Charitable Trust enabled purchase of the facility, which hosts exchange programs with Oxford colleges and universities and hosts spring and summer study abroad programs. The emphasis on international education outlined in 1988 was clearly successful, as by 2005 nearly 150 students participated in annual study abroad programs, supported by scholarships totaling more than $150,000.

The Spencer House in Oxford, England is the home of the CSU in Oxford program.

The stairs at the corner of University Avenue and Gentian Boulevard greet visitors to the main campus.

The college also reached out to visitors overseas, creating the English Language Institute in 1993 to provide language and culture training to international students. In 1996, the participants of the English Language Institute from Kiryu, Japan, funded the construction of the Kiryu Garden adjacent to the Richards Building. The garden is a living symbol of the ongoing relationship between Columbus and its sister city and is also an acknowledgement of the impact of the college on the lives of the residents of Kiryu. The successor of the English Language Institute, the American Language Program, remains a successful program and continues to assist international visitors with English language competency and to offer an opportunity for cultural immersion in the United States.

Enrollment rebounded in the early 1990s, making Columbus College one of the fastest-growing institutions in the state between 1988 and 1995. Even with increased enrollment and expanded

Cody Road became University Avenue in October 1993.
(Photograph by Reagan L. Grimsley)

assisted the college in shedding the "Cody Road High" label and also proved to be a precursor to the eagerly anticipated change to university status. The extension of the roadway to Manchester Expressway also provided an easier approach to campus, and in 1993 work began on a project to erect a new main entrance to campus. The new entrance streamlined access from University Avenue, and the later addition of a brick stairway at the corner of University and Gentian provided an aesthetic guidepost by which to identify the campus.

Although the roadway proclaimed university status, official recognition from the state was still not forthcoming. In 1990, the college entered a concerted effort to move from college to university status, making goal number one of the strategic plan to become a university. The rationale, as outlined in the 1990 Columbus College Annual Report, was simple: "University status would enhance the College's competitive position in the recruitment of faculty and students, its external and internal images, and its ability to attract higher levels of federal and private support." For half a decade, the Board of Regents of the University System of Georgia resisted a name change for two main reasons. First, the structure of the university system contained no provisions for a designation between a college with undergraduate programs and a regional university. Since several state colleges actively sought university status in the early 1990s, a concern existed at the Board of Regents that too many universities would weaken the hierarchy of the system. Second, the early 1990s were also lean budget years, and if schools elevated to university status required increased program funding, the resources were not available to support a change.

By 1996, however, it was clear the Board of Regents would finally address the issue by creating a new tier in the system between state college and regional university. This new tier would recognize twelve Georgia Board of Regents institutions as state universities, or institutions that granted undergraduate and master's level degrees. In an interview with the *Columbus*

facilities, the college administration faced an uphill battle in attaining university status from the Board of Regents of the University System of Georgia. Columbus College was one of a number of institutions requesting a change in status, including neighboring Albany State College, Fort Valley State College, Georgia Southwestern College, and West Georgia College. By 1993, students enrolling at Columbus College were not only from Columbus and Muscogee County, but increasingly from the adjoining Chattahoochee Valley region of Georgia and Alabama.

This evolution of the college into a regional institution represented an important landmark in the growth of the college. Even though the school retained its close ties with the local community, it was no longer a small junior college on the outskirts of Columbus. Illustrating this change was the renaming of Cody Road—effective October 1, 1993, the thruway officially became University Avenue. While subtle, this change in terminology greatly

*Ledger-Enquirer* on June 11, 1996, Chancellor Stephen R. Portch explained the decision: "When I talked to a lot of people around the state, what their real interest was in was not regional university status per se and additional programs and budget. What was really pushing their desire was to have an appropriate name for their students and their institution."

Passed on June 12, 1996, the new designation transformed Columbus College into Columbus State University. On September 25, 1996, the campus and community took part in a celebration of the new status under the spire of the clock tower. Recognizing the importance of the occasion, Columbus Mayor Bobby Peters, himself a two-time college alumnus, announced that the Columbus

The Frank G. Lumpkin, Jr. Center opened on November 27, 2000. The sports complex occupies ninety-six thousand square feet and seats forty-five hundred. (Photograph by Reagan L. Grimsley)

City Council designated September 19–25, 1996, as Columbus State University Week. The new name and status validated the growth and expansion of the university. One faculty member interviewed by the Columbus State University *Saber* on October 3, 1996, commented, "It should have happened a long time ago. It (CSU) has been functioning as such for so many years."

The elevation to university status was not the only major change on campus in the decade, however. In 1995, Chancellor Portch presented a plan to move all Board of Regents institutions from the quarter plan of enrollment to a two-semester academic year. Approved on December 13, 1995, by the Board of Regents, the change from four quarters to two semesters and a summer session would take effect in August 1998. This change represented a major reorganization of the academic calendar for the campus, as the four equally distributed quarters of fall, winter, spring, and summer shifted to two full semesters during fall and spring and a shorter summer semester.

Three other significant developments took place at the university in 1998. First, the four major schools of the university, Arts and Letters, Science, Education, and Business, became colleges to better align their position with the nascent university status. Second, Columbus State University added a fifth college, University College, to promote basic skills development and to offer remedial courses for students. The third major development was the addition of an Honors Program to challenge outstanding students. As the dawn of a new century neared, Columbus State University positioned itself as a regional leader in undergraduate and graduate education, a status it would solidify over the next eight years.

The first years of the new millennium were exciting times for the university. Building on a tradition of achievement, CSU athletic teams competed successfully on both regional and national levels. The school's entry into the NCAA Division II Peach Belt Conference in 1990 helped establish rivalries with schools in Georgia, Florida, and South Carolina, and led to the development of a range of highly competitive athletic programs for men and women. Playing in a new home, the Frank G. Lumpkin, Jr. Center, both the women's and men's basketball teams reached new heights in the twenty-first century. The highly successful baseball team, already a national contender, added the title of national champion to its repertoire of honors in this decade. The CSU cheerleaders and men's golf also produced national champions in the first decade of the century.

Built in 1962 and opened in 1963, the Woodruff Gym initially served the college well as the home of athletics. By the 1990s, however, it was evident that the college needed a new home for its physical education and athletic departments. The aging building, while serviceable, was a liability for recruiting quality athletes. The dream of a new physical education complex became reality in 1998, with groundbreaking held for the building on October 10 of the same year. The project received a major donation from former insurance executive Frank Lumpkin, Jr. in June 1999, when he donated two million dollars to the project. Named in honor of Lumpkin, the state-of-the-art ninety-six-thousand-square-foot arena with seating for forty-five hundred people opened on November 27, 2000. The complex is also home to twenty-one offices, eight locker rooms, a jogging/walking track, a spacious conference room, and a sports medicine and training room. The Columbus State University Athletic Hall of Fame, founded in 1996, relocated to the mezzanine of the building. The Hall of Fame honors outstanding members of the CSU community who contributed to the success of the university's athletic program. In addition to hosting athletic events, the Lumpkin Center serves the campus in a variety of capacities, including hosting university meetings and graduation.

In the season preceding the opening of the Lumpkin Center, the Lady Cougar basketball team reached the Elite Eight of the NCAA Division II tournament, gaining national recognition for a young program founded in 1989 under Head Coach Jay Sparks. In 2000–2001, the Lady Cougars completed the regular season with a perfect 28-0 record, finishing the season ranked number one in NCAA Division II. The team recorded a 31-0 record before reaching the national semifinals and being eliminated by eventual national champions Cal Poly Pomona. While falling just short of a national title, the achievements of the young women were remarkable for a program with such a brief history. The team has four times won or shared the Peach Belt Conference Regular Season Championship and regularly appears in the NCAA Division II national tournament, with the most recent visit occurring in 2006-2007.

The 2000–2001 Lady Cougar basketball team finished the season with a record of 31-1, with the only loss coming in the NCAA Division II semi-final game.

The men's basketball team reached a higher plateau in the first decade of the new century as well. Coach Herbert Greene's Cougars began a streak of thirteen consecutive winning seasons in 1993–1994, winning four Peach Belt regular season titles in the process. The Cougars also consistently appeared in the NCAA Division II national tournament, starting a string of four consecutive appearances in the 2002–2003 season. In 2006, Herbert Greene retired from coaching after two-and-

a-half decades to focus on his position as athletic director. After a 17-12 season under interim Coach Doug Branson in 2006–2007, the former Greene assistant was named the permanent head basketball coach in the spring of 2007.

The crowning achievement in athletics at Columbus State was the 2002 NCAA Division II national championship in baseball. After thirty stellar years on the diamond, the team reached the pinnacle of success under Coach Greg Appleton. Playing their

The 2002 Cougar baseball team celebrates after winning the NCAA Division II national championship in Montgomery, Alabama.

home games at Ragsdale Field, which was renovated and improved in 1989 and 1996, the team recorded 48 wins and 15 losses in their championship season. The team revisited the College World Series in 2004 and 2007, reaching the national championship game in 2007 before falling to the University of Tampa.

Other university sports also gained notice during the new decade. The CSU golf team added a chapter to its long and storied history in 2007 when golfer Christian Ries became the sixth Cougar golfer to capture an individual NCAA Division II national championship. In addition to the six individual national champions, the team claimed national champion honors six times, in 1978, 1980, 1989, 1992, 1994, and 1997.

Under the direction of Jimbo Davis, the CSU cheer squads regularly contend for national championships, bringing home two UCA National Championships and seven Peach Belt titles. The Columbus State women's soccer team began play in 2004 under the leadership of Coach Jay Entlich. The team won a Peach Belt Conference title in its second year of existence and secured a Peach Belt Tournament title in 2006. The women advanced to the NCAA Division II Southeastern Region tournament in 2006, achieving a top-ten ranking along the way. In 2007, the women's softball team advanced to the NCAA Division II championship tournament and finished the season 3rd in the nation with a 58-5 record. Each of these programs strives for excellence, and as a result Columbus State University received the 2005–2006 and 2006–2007 Commissioner's Cup as the top overall athletic program in the Peach Belt Conference.

As the Lumpkin Center neared completion as the home of athletics, a multi-purpose performing arts complex was also receiving its finishing touches in downtown Columbus. One of the key components of Dr. Frank Brown's inaugural speech in 1988 was for the university to strive for excellence in the arts and humanities. Building on the bedrock of a regionally recognized music department, the university partnered with the local community to raise more than a hundred million dollars for local arts projects, including construction of the RiverCenter for the Performing Arts in uptown Columbus. A majority of these funds came from the Columbus Challenge, a public-private

Christian Ries continued the tradition of excellence established by the men's golf team, winning the individual NCAA Division II national championship in 2007. The men's golf team has won six team national championships, and the school boasts six individual national champions as well.

The RiverCenter for the Performing Arts opened in 2001. The Schwob School of Music and the CSU Music Library are located in the complex.

The Genesis Gospel Choir performs in RiverCenter's Legacy Hall. Genesis is one of a number of student-led campus groups which enrich life at CSU. (Photograph by Terri A. Kimble)

The Schwob School of Music offers outstanding programs, attracting students from across the nation and around the world. Students Marquis Hare, Hisa Fujino, and Nicholas Greer pose for a snapshot after a jazz concert on the lawn of the RiverCenter. (Photograph by Terri A. Kimble)

fundraising campaign designed to construct and renovate key cultural complexes in the city. Completed in 2001, the state-of-the-art building contains three performance venues and houses the Columbus State University Schwob School of Music and the Columbus State University Music Library. Administered by the Georgia Department of Natural Resources, the RiverCenter not only hosts many Schwob School of Music performances, but also attracts major performing artists from across the nation and around the world. To support the uptown student population, the Columbus State University Foundation acquired the former Rankin Hotel and adjacent properties. The Rankin transformed into the Rankin Arts Center, home of a number of continuing education programs in the arts, as well as student housing for those based downtown. This was the first major step toward creating an uptown fine and performing arts campus for the university.

Another capital campaign would accelerate the completion of the downtown campus. Columbus College built solidly on the successful Campaign for Excellence in 1984–1985, creating a healthy annual giving program in 1992 named the Annual Fund, with its signature event of Columbus College Day, now CSU Day. The Tower Society, a group of college alumni who donate in excess of a thousand dollars per year, also formed during the early 1990s, and the financial support of the members of this group is instrumental in providing scholarships at the university. Through these and other gifts, by 2001 the local community proved that it supported Columbus State. Still, to achieve its full potential, the institution embarked on a second major capital campaign. Under the direction of Campaign Chairman Jimmy Yancey, the effort, themed an Investment in People, initially sought to raise sixty-seven million dollars. By the time canvassing closed on October 31, 2005, some twenty-five hundred donors pledged more than a hundred million dollars to enhance four areas of need: Learning and Service, Teacher Preparation, Arts and Culture, and Technology and Commerce. Thirty donors offered gifts exceeding one million dollars, with the largest single gift, $25

million, coming from the Bradley-Turner Foundation. Gifts to the university created thirty-six endowed scholarships for students, nine endowed faculty chairs, initiatives to recruit and support Hispanic and Latino students, the Saunders Center for Music Studies, and the Carson McCullers Center for Writers and Musicians. Large donations bolstered funding for faculty development, the CSU Servant Leadership Program, and the teacher mentoring

CSU alumnus Jimmy Yancey led the Investment in People capital campaign, which raised more than a hundred million dollars to support the university.

program. Major contributions also led to new building projects, including the Cunningham Center for Leadership Development and the Schuster Student Success Center. The outcome resonated throughout the community, proving that Columbus State University remained an institution of higher learning supported solidly by local residents. Campaign Chairman Jimmy Yancey summed up the effort: "The common element of this campaign is people—those with vision who developed the plan, those who will implement it, those who will benefit from it and those whose support will make it all possible."

One of the plans made possible by the support was the construction of an expanded uptown campus, dubbed the

The CSU RiverPark campus expanded dramatically in 2006. The Theatre on the Park and the Corn Center for the Visual Arts are two key components of the complex.

Students rehearse for *A Midsummer Night's Dream*, the first production in the new Theatre on the Park.

RiverPark campus. Expanded housing options, a new theatre building, a renovated facility to house the visual arts, and office and administrative space for the departments of art and theatre were all part of the master plan for the new campus. In the spring of 2007, the Theatre on the Park, the Corn Center for the Visual Arts, and the Yancey Center welcomed their first students to downtown. The Theatre on the Park, the performance home for the CSU theatre department, is located overlooking the Chattahoochee River in downtown Columbus. Its sister building, the Corn Center for the Visual Arts, is located in a renovated warehouse and contains classroom and gallery space for the arts. The Yancey Center contains classrooms and faculty

The Yancey Center at One Arsenal Place on the RiverPark campus houses offices, classrooms, and student activity space for the art and theatre departments.

offices for both the art and theatre departments. By 2007, the RiverPark campus provided housing for 350 Columbus State University students. In combination with the RiverCenter for the Performing Arts, these new facilities are evidence that the vision for excellence in the fine and performing arts at Columbus State University is no longer a dream, but a reality.

Fine and performing arts students can learn, live, and relax on the RiverPark campus. Here art students sketch on a downtown greenspace. Broadway Crossing, one of the two newest student apartment buildings, is pictured in the background.

In August 2007, President Frank Brown announced his retirement from Columbus State University, effective June 30, 2008. Looking back over the two decades he served at the helm of the institution, vast changes are evident. In 1988, then Columbus College enrolled fewer than four thousand students; by 2007 that number soared to more than seventy-five hundred. After a lengthy struggle, the college gained university status, and as the new century dawned, Columbus State University expanded to three locations, two in Columbus and one in Oxford, England. Collaborative projects yielded the Coca-Cola Space Science Center, Oxbow Meadows Environmental Learning Center, and a nationally

renowned program for technology training in conjunction with Total Systems and Aflac. A resoundingly successful Investment in People campaign provided funding for a wide range of projects, including buildings for art and theatre and the Cunningham Conference Center on the main campus. A stellar program in

Actor Sidney Poitier and CSU President Frank Brown discuss the new RiverPark facilities.

international education allows for an extensive array of learning opportunities, including study abroad and visiting scholar programs. Athletic teams enjoyed national recognition, and CSU produced national champions and played in an outstanding new athletic facility. Campus housing expanded to accommodate more than a thousand students, creating a substantial residential base for the previously all-commuter school. Continued excellence in biology, education, nursing, and business offer students a variety of career paths.

At the heart of these initiatives, however, Brown guided the entire university community with two major goals in mind: providing students with the best possible learning experience

CSU students often contribute to the community. In 2004–2005, student organizations and the Servant Leadership program banded together to fund and build a Habitat for Humanity home in Columbus. (Photograph by Terri A. Kimble)

and ensuring that Columbus State University retained the community roots from which it sprang fifty years earlier. In his own words, Brown views success in much simpler terms, referring to "Columbus State University as being a place where we take

our greatest satisfaction in lives changed, opportunities provided, dreams accomplished, and futures brightened." The future is indeed bright, as the university is poised to continue a fifty-year tradition of changing and enriching lives.

Welcome Back Week is held each fall. Students Jessica Espada of Westminster Fellowship, and John Cooper of the Baptist Student Union, recruit new members and have a little fun during the Welcome Back Picnic, 2004. (Photograph by Terri A. Kimble)

CSU is part of a national network of colleges and schools. After the tragic shootings at Virginia Tech University in 2007, CSU paid tribute to the victims, and students signed this banner to send to the Blacksburg campus. (Photograph by Reagan L. Grimsley)

The staff of Computer Information and Network Services, pictured here at the groundbreaking for the Center for Commerce and Technology, is crucial to the success of the university

Staff gather at the Thomas Y. Whitley Clock Tower for coffee and doughnuts, an event sponsored by the Staff Council. (Photograph by Terri A. Kimble)

The dedicated university staff is key to keeping the institution running smoothly. Pictured are, left to right, Maria Holmes, Wanda Crowe, Patsy Redmond, and Sharon May.

College life has changed a great deal in fifty years, and students now use a mixture of traditional and current technology as they complete degree requirements.

CSU Day celebrates those who support the CSU Annual Fund by delivering a variety of goodies to contributors, including "We are Partners With CSU" yard signs.

Alumni are active on campus, as demonstrated by volunteers at the alumni tent on Move-In Day. Alumni, faculty, and staff lend campus residents a hand in settling into their apartments.

Community outreach remains an important part of the CSU mission. Former National Basketball Association Hall of Fame member Julius Erving, known by his nickname "Dr. J," gives an inspirational speech to participants at the CSU Lady Cougar Team Camp in 2005.

The Cunningham Center for Leadership Development, located on the site of the former President's home, opened in 2004. The late John Cunningham donated over $4 million to fund construction of the facility. (Photograph by Reagan L. Grimsley)

Dr. Martha D. Saunders served as vice president for academic affairs from 2002 until 2005. She is one of four former vice presidents for academic affairs to go on to become college or university presidents. She is currently the president of the University of Southern Mississippi.

# Bibliography

Chappell, Delane. *An Enduring Presence: A History of the Public Library in Columbus, Georgia.* Columbus, Georgia: Chattahoochee Regional Library System, 2005.

*Saber.* The Newspaper of Columbus College and Columbus State University, 1958-2007.

Columbus College *Grey and Gold,* 1958-1959.

Columbus College *Sentry,* 1960-1972.

Columbus State University Scrapbooks, Columbus State University Archives, Columbus State University, Columbus, Georgia.

Davidson, J.Q. "Columbus College Commencement Address, June 7, 1965." Typescript copy located in Columbus State University Collection, Columbus State University, Columbus, Georgia.

England, James W. Sr. "The Quest for a Community College: The Birth of Columbus College." Unpublished paper, Columbus State University Collection, Columbus State University, Columbus, Georgia.

Fincher, Cameron. *The Historical Development of the University System of Georgia, 1932–1990.* Athens, Georgia: Institute of Higher Education, 1991.

"Francis J. Brooke." Interview published in the *Columbus Magazine,* Volume 2, No. 3: May/June 1983, 29, 31.

Lloyd, Craig. *Columbus College: Reaching for Tomorrow.* Columbus, Georgia: Columbus College, 1983.

Lloyd, Craig. "Columbus State University." Entry in the New Georgia Encyclopedia located online at http://www.georgiaencyclopedia.org.

Lloyd, Craig. *Their Time, Their Influence, Their Substance: The Story of the Columbus College Foundation, 1963–1993.* Columbus, Georgia, Columbus College, 1993.

Lloyd, Craig. "The Origins and Development of Columbus College." Proceedings and Papers of the Georgia Association of Historians, Volume 6, 1985: 24-31.

Lupold, John S. *Columbus, Georgia, 1828-1978.* Columbus, Georgia: Columbus Sesquicentennial Inc, 1978.

Mahan, Katherine and W. C. Woodall. *History of Public Schools in Columbus, Muscogee County, Georgia, 1828–1976.* Columbus, Georgia: Muscogee County Board of Education, 1976.

McGee, Billy D. "Twenty-Five Years and Growing: A History of Columbus College Athletics, 1958–1983." Unpublished paper, Columbus State University Collection, Columbus State University Archives, Columbus, Georgia.

Mock, Lindsey. Oral History interview conducted by Kimberly Stokes Pak, February 24, 2007. Columbus State University Archives, Columbus State University, Columbus, Georgia.

Rothschild, Jac. "Dedication Address at Columbus College, June 1, 1969." Typescript copy located in Columbus State University Collection, Columbus State University Archives, Columbus, Georgia.

Shaw, William Henry. "Historical Development of Columbus College." Speech delivered on January 6, 1963 in Columbus, Georgia. Typescript copy located in Columbus State University Archives Collection, Columbus State University, Columbus, Georgia.

Stanley, T. Hiram. "First Commencement Address of Columbus College, June 5, 1960." Typescript copy located in Columbus State University Collection, Columbus State University, Columbus, Georgia.

Whitley, Thomas Y. Oral History interviews conducted by Craig Lloyd, November 19, 1982 and December 6, 1982, Columbus State University Archives, Columbus State University, Columbus, Georgia.

# Appendix I    Original Columbus College Faculty and Staff

Thomas Y. Whitley, A.B., M.S., Ed.D      President

## Faculty

Philip Battle, B.A., M.A.      Social Science, Spanish
Wimberly E. Brown, A.B., A.M.      History
Dewey B. Cash, B.S. M. Ed.      Mathematics
Lucia C. Green, B.A., M.L.      Librarian
Blackshear T. Hartley, Jr., A.B. M. Ed.      English
Glen W. Herrin, A.B., M.S.      Business Administration
William Howard, B.A., M.S.      English
Nora Killian, A.B., M.S.      Biology
Katherine H. Mahan, B.M., M.M.      English, Music
Alvin L. McLendon, Jr., B.A., M.A., M.S.      Mathematics, Physics
Kenneth Nance, B.S. A.M.      Biology, Chemistry
Donothan C. Olliff, B.A., M.A.      Political Science
Celia B. Taylor, B.S., M.A.      English, Speech
Frank C. Townsend, B.S., M.A.      Physical Education

## Staff

Pauline Banks      Secretary to the President
Doyle M. Dillard      Comptroller
Rosemary Duncan      Secretary
Mary L. Livengood      Counselor, Registrar
Lois Thompson      Bookkeeper

The first faculty of Columbus College are pictured in this 1958 image.

A newly hired administration and staff greeted students when they enrolled for the first classes at Columbus College in 1958. Pictured in the bottom row, left to right, are Lois Thompson, Pauline C. Banks, and Rosemary Duncan. In the top row are Dr. Thomas Y. Whitley, Mary L. Livengood, and Doyle M. Dillard.

# The First Graduating Class of Columbus College

## Appendix II

**Degrees Awarded on June 5, 1960**

John Aubrey Baggett

Max Eugene Baggett

Lewis E. Bailess

Linda Anne Bandy

Cynthia Adelaide Betts

David Wendell Blackshear*

Judith Elaine Braswell

Carolyn Helen Crowder

Dorothy Jean David

Douglas Howard Dorough

Harry R. Fischer

Carl W. Franklin

Georgia Ann Garrett

Judith Ray Grimes

Gloria Sue Huguley

Sylvia Helene Kunzig*

James Allen Lane

Nancy L. Langford*

Marlene Elmore Melvin*

Billy E. Moore

Mary Elizabeth Moore

Willice Ralph Mullins II

J. Wade Munford, Jr.

Beverly Pauline Noel

Shirley A. Parker

Thomas H. Richburg

Ruth LaDue Scott*

Jerry H. Sewell

Raymond W. Tibbits, Jr.

Myrtle Ann Tucker

**Those graduating with high honors are noted with an asterisk.**

# Appendix III    Award-Winning Faculty, Staff, and Students

## Faculty
### Distinguished Professor Award (original award)

| | |
|---|---|
| 1963–1964 | Dr. Larry Lupo, Associate Professor of History |
| 1964–1965 | Dr. Benjamin Bailey, History |
| 1965–1966 | Ms. Dorothy Hatfield, Assistant Professor of English |
| 1966–1967 | Ms. Anne Stearns, Chemistry |
| 1967–1968 | Dr. Richard Amundson, Associate Professor of History |
| 1968–1969 | Mr. Billy McGee, Assistant Professor of History |
| 1969–1970 | Mr. James Chappel, Assistant Professor of English |
| 1970–1971 | Dr. J. William Rooney, Associate Professor of History |
| 1971–1972 | Dr. William Gerlach, Associate Professor of Political Science |
| 1972–1973 | Dr. George Stanton, Associate Professor of Biology |
| 1973–1974 | Dr. Nam Yearl Chai, Associate Professor of Political Science |
| 1974–1975 | Mr. Ronald Gray, Instructor of Accounting |
| 1975–1976 | Dr. Richard Amundson, Professor of History |

### Outstanding Educator Award (replaced Distinguished Professor Award)

| | |
|---|---|
| 1976–1977 | Ms. Jackie Titus, Associate Professor of Mental Health |
| 1977–1978 | Dr. Joel Horowitz, Associate Professor of Sociology |
| 1978–1979 | Dr. Thornton Jordan, Professor of English |
| 1979–1980 | Dr. Nam Yearl Chai, Professor of Political Science |
| 1980–1981 | Dr. Paul J. Vander Gheynst, Professor of Music |
| 1981–1982 | Dr. Terry Norris, Professor of Criminal Justice |
| 1982–1983 | Dr. Francis Gardner, Professor of Biology |
| 1983–1984 | Dr. Virginia Carr, Professor of English |

### Educator of the Year (replaced Outstanding Educator Award)

| | |
|---|---|
| 1984–1985 | Dr. William J. Frazier, Professor of Biology |
| 1985–1986 | Ms. Mary Jane Wadkins, Associate Professor of History |

| 1986–1987 | Dr. Sandra M. Hortman, Associate Professor of Marketing |
| 1987–1988 | Dr. John B. Myers, Professor of History |
| 1988–1989 | Dr. William Birkhead, Professor of Biology |
| 1989–1990 | Dr. Mario Mion, Professor of Political Science |
| 1990–1991 | Mr. David Johnson, Professor of English |
| 1991–1992 | Dr. Phillip Green, Assistant Professor of Political Science |
| 1992–1993 | Dr. Sandra M. Hortman, Associate Professor of Marketing |
| 1993–1994 | Dr. Mary Schild, Professor of Psychology |
| 1994–1995 | Mr. David Johnson, Professor of English |
| 1995–1996 | Ms. Beverly Davis, Assistant Professor of Learning Support Mathematics |
| 1996–1997 | Dr. John Lupold, Professor of History |
| 1997–1998 | Dr. Joseph McIntosh, Professor of Health Science |
| 1998–1999 | Dr. Shawn Cruzen, Associate Professor of Astronomy |
| 1999–2000 | Dr. Glenn Stokes, Professor of Biology |
| 2000–2001 | Dr. Harvey Richman, Associate Professor of Psychology |
| 2001–2002 | Ms. Tamara S. Bollis-Pecci, Assistant Professor of Communication |
| 2002–2003 | Dr. Julie Ann Ballenger, Professor of Biology |
| 2003–2004 | Dr. Shawn Cruzen, Associate Professor of Astronomy |
| 2004–2005 | Dr. Peter S. Brown, Professor of Art History |
| 2005–2006 | Dr. Richard L. Newtson, Associate Professor Sociology and Gerontology |
| 2006–2007 | Dr. Dorinda Dowis, Associate Professor of Criminal Justice |

## Faculty Research and Scholarship Award

| 1994–1995 | Dr. David Schwimmer, Professor of Geology |
| 1995–1996 | Dr. Zeki Y. Al-Saigh, Professor of Chemistry |
| 1996–1997 | Dr. Johnny Ho, Professor of Management |
| 1997–1998 | Dr. William S. Birkhead, Professor of Biology |
| 1998–1999 | Dr. Mary Lindquist, Fuller E. Callaway Professor of Mathematics Education |
| 1999–2000 | Dr. James A. Gore, Professor of Environmental Science |
| 2000–2001 | Dr. Craig Lloyd, Professor of History/Archivist |
| 2001–2002 | Dr. Mark Thornton, Associate Professor of Economics |
| 2002–2003 | Dr. David Schwimmer, Professor of Geology |
| 2003–2004 | Dr. Johnny Ho, Professor of Management |
| | Dr. Bhagyavati, Professor of Computer Science |
| 2005–2006 | Mr. Reagan L. Grimsley, Assistant Professor Library Science/Archivist |
| 2006–2007 | Dr. Jeff Kaller, Associate Professor of Art |

## Vice President's Award (original award)

| | |
|---|---|
| 1981–1982 | Mr. James H. Chappel, Professor of English |
| 1982–1983 | Dr. Dorothy Sutherland, Associate Professor of Communicative Disorders |
| 1983–1984 | Dr. Frances M. Duncan, Professor of Education |
| 1984–1985 | Dr. George E. Stanton, Professor of Biology |

## Faculty Service Award (replaced VP's Award)

| | |
|---|---|
| 1985–1986 | Dr. John Myers, Professor of History |
| 1986–1987 | Dr. James B. McCollum, Professor of Economics |
| 1987–1988 | Dr. Richard J. Amundson, Professor of History |
| 1988–1989 | Dr. J. Kitt Lumley, Professor of Mathematics |
| 1989–1990 | Ms. Jackie K. Titus, Associate Professor of Mental Health |
| 1990–1991 | Mr. James H. Chappel, Professor of English |
| 1991–1992 | Dr. John S. Lupold, Professor of History |
| 1992–1993 | Dr. Tom Wentland, Professor of Developmental Studies |
| 1993–1994 | Dr. Jaynie Nesmith, Associate Professor of Education |
| 1994–1995 | Dr. Sandra K. Stratford, Associate Professor of Library Science |
| 1995–1996 | Dr. Harold Whitman, Professor of Education |
| 1996–1997 | Dr. Rochelle Ripple, Professor of Education |
| 1997–1998 | Dr. Michaell Taylor, Professor of Recreation/Physical Education |
| 1998–1999 | Dr. William Chappell, Professor of Political Science |
| 1999–2000 | Dr. Francis E. Gardner, Professor of Biology |
| 2000–2001 | Dr. Sallie D. Averitt-Miller, Associate Professor of Reading Education |
| 2001–2002 | Dr. J. Alyce Cook, Associate Professor of Spanish |
| 2002–2003 | Dr. Teresa S. Irvin, Associate Professor of Writing Instruction |
| 2003–2004 | Dr. Thomas P. Loughman, Professor of Business Administration |
| 2004–2005 | Dr. Deborah Gober, Professor of Math Education |
| 2005–2006 | Dr. William James Owen, Associate Professor English |
| 2006–2007 | Dr. Daniel Ross, Professor of English |

## Staff

### Employee of the Year

1992  Nancy Duncan
1993  Rebecca Boswell
1994  Wynell King
1995  Denise Cotton

### Staff Service Award

1998  Glen Ketterlinus
1999  Christi Dixon

### Cougar Pride Award

2004  Loave Todd
2005  Jon Haney
2006  Patsy Redmond

## Students

### Faculty Cup

1960  Carl W. Franklin
1961  Carolyn G. Martin
1962  John L. Quick
1963  Guerry M. Thode
1964  James E. Hurstson
1965  Carol A. Skinner
1966  Ronald M. Hudson
1967  Ronnie L. Patterson
1968  Nancy K. Carr
1969  Susan L. Mercer
1970  Lon D. Marlowe III
1971  Geraldine I. Paul
1972  Joseph N. Herren
1973  Ben L. Tucker
1974  Robert P. Morpeth
1975  Deborah L. Braun
1976  John R. Trotter
1977  Jerry A. Jenkins
1978  Nancy Allison Carter
      Diane Walker
1979  Karen S. Clark
1980  Bernice B. Dean
      Jeanette L. Colson
1981  Emilie Alison Slade
1982  Denise A. Yardley
1983  Robin R. Hallums
1984  Perry E. Jones
1985  Jami M. Norris
1986  David R. Travis
1987  Lisa M. Pharis
      Timothy P. Randolph
1988  James W. England, Sr.
1989  Ann Marie Manning

| | | |
|---|---|---|
| 1990 | Susan B. Jones | |
| 1991 | Jennifer B. Dickerson | |
| 1992 | Mickey J. Stoneback | |
| 1993 | Kenneth E. Evans, Jr. | |
| 1994 | Jason D. Mizell | |
| 1995 | Shannon E. Flanagan | |
| 1996 | Susan M. McCullum | |
| 1997 | Michelle L. Miller | |
| 1998 | Joel Judah | |
| 1999 | Anna Mion | |
| 2000 | Antoinette H. Mion | |
| 2001 | Chad M. Andrae | |
| 2002 | Jacquelynn M. Jordan | |
| 2003 | Mary E. Hill | |
| 2004 | Katharine A. Cannella | |
| 2005 | Courtney Blayke Gibson | |
| 2006 | Melissa L. McDaniel | |
| 2007 | Nicole de Vries | |

## Eason Leadership Award

| | |
|---|---|
| 2001 | Rekha Daswani |
| 2002 | Robin Remich |
| 2003 | Candace Turner |
| 2004 | Cathleen Kirkland |
| 2005 | Lucas Loureiro |
| 2006 | Leonard Moore |
| 2007 | Nicole de Vries |

# Alumni

## Thomas Y. Whitley Distinguished Alumnus Award

| | |
|---|---|
| 1980 | Charles R. Eason, '72 |
| 1981 | Helen T. Milian, '61 |
| 1982 | James A. Gill, '71 |
| 1983 | Nancy C. Buntin, '68 |
| 1984 | Wm. Jim Wetherington, '74 |
| 1985 | James F. Loudermilk, '70 |
| 1986 | Wallace A. Kite, '74 |
| 1987 | James D. Yancey, '64 |
| 1988 | Carole L. Rutland, '72 |
| 1989 | Sharon O. Sudderth, '79 |
| 1990 | Peggy H. Batastini, '73 |
| 1991 | Kenneth E. Evans, '70 |
| 1992 | C. Jackie Farris, '76 |
| 1993 | Mary Jane Wadkins, '70 |
| 1994 | L. Lamar Powers, '70 |
| 1995 | James H. Motos, '66 |
| 1996 | Rick C. Gordon, '76 |
| 1997 | Michael W. Patrick, '73 |
| 1998 | Don Andrae, '70 |
| 1999 | Evelyn W. Turner, '77 |
| 2000 | Richard A. Smith, '75 |
| 2001 | Dell W. McMullen, '73 |
| 2002 | Wm. D. Reaves, Jr., '66 |
| 2003 | Emory J. Alexander, '74 |
| 2004 | Sherree W. Mitchell, '75 |
| 2005 | Linda U. Hadley, '80 |
| 2006 | Troy Woods, '74 |

Geri Paul receives the Faculty Cup from dean Wimberly Brown. Also pictured are faculty members Dr. Hugh Rodgers, Dr. Nemia Chai, and Patricia Spano.

Charles Eason receives the first Dr. Thomas Y. Whitley Distinguished Alumnus Award from Jack Brinkley. The Eason Leadership Scholarship is named in his honor.

Susan Mercer, Faculty Cup recipient, celebrates with Professor Billy McGee, named Educator of the Year in 1969.

Dr. Frank D. Brown with 1998–1999 award winners Dr. William Chappell, Anna Mion, Dr. Shawn Cruzen, and Dr. Mary Lindquist.

The *Saber* announces the 1969 winners of the Faculty Cup and Top Professor awards.

Lucus Loureiro, winner of the 2005 Charles Eason Leadership Award. An international student from Brazil, Loureiro served as Student Government Association president and was a visiting student at Oxford. (Photograph by Terri A. Kimble)

Mary Hill Johnson, 2003 graduate of Columbus State University and winner of the Faculty Cup, returned to the university in the fall of 2007 to present the keynote address at Freshman Convocation.

Dean Linda Hadley of the D. Abbott Turner College of Business received the Dr. Thomas Y. Whitley Distinguished Alumnus Award in 2005. Hadley successfully guided her college to accreditation by the Association to Advance Collegiate Schools of Business in 2004, a designation achieved by less than twenty-seven percent of the business schools in the United States.

Dr. John S. Lupold received the Educator of the Year Award and the Faculty Service Award during his career at the college.

| | |
|---|---|
| *Adams, Olin B. (1960) | Associate Professor, History |
| Adams, Paulette (1975) | Professor, Early Childhood Education |
| *Amundson, Richard J. (1966) | Professor, History |
| Anderson, John H. (1969) | Professor, Music |
| Angermuller, Sarah (1976) | Associate Professor, Nursing |
| Arno, Elsie R. (1975) | Associate Professor, Economics |
| Atkins, James T. (1974) | Professor, Education |
| Bagley, Earl G. (1973) | Associate Professor, Social Science Education |
| *Bailey, Benjamin F. (1963) | Professor, History |
| Batastini, Peggy H. (1973) | Associate Professor, Nursing |
| Berger, Elinor E. (1971) | Professor, Mathematics |
| Berger, Mark L. (1970) | Professor, History |
| Blackmon, Mary V. (1959) | Professor, Physical Education |
| Bohannon, John L. (1970) | Associate Professor, Finance |
| *Brown, Jack A. (1962) | Professor, English |
| Brown, Wimberly E. (1958) | Professor, Associate Director, Student Services |
| Caproni, Bettyesue R. (1976) | Associate Professor, Nursing |
| Carlisle, Earnest (1969) | Professor, Mathematics Education |
| Cartledge, Carolyn M. (1976) | Professor, Education |
| Cash, Dewey B. (1958) | Professor Mathematics |
| Chai, Nemia M. (1965) | Professor, Language and Literature |
| Chappel, James H. (1966) | Professor, English |
| Clark, Flora M. (1971) | Professor, Biology |
| Clark, Neil P. (1969) | Professor, Science Education |
| Clements, Frank M. (1959) | Professor, Physical Education |
| Cook, Cline G. (1979) | Associate Professor, Finance |
| Cope, Donald A. (1968) | Associate Professor, History |
| Crim, John W. (1977) | Professor, Management |
| Davidson, Judy K. (1971) | Associate Professor, Chair, Nursing |

| | |
|---|---|
| Duncan, Frances M. (1970) | Professor, Mental Retardation |
| *Dwyer, James J. (1968) | Associate Professor, History |
| *Ford, H. Thomas (1996) | Professor, Exercise Science and Physical Education |
| Friedman, Lenemaja V. (1969) | Professor, English |
| Gardner, Jr., Francis E. (1974) | Professor, Biology |
| George, Joseph D. (1973) | Professor, Specific Learning Disabilities |
| Gibson, Hal J. (1976) | Professor, Music |
| *Gibson, Richard G. (1982) | Professor, Chair Mathematics |
| Gonzalez, Raymond B. (1969) | Professor, Political Science |
| *Grimson, Jr., Keith S. (1977) | Professor, Art |
| *Hackett, Paul T. (1970) | Associate Professor, English |
| Hall-Brennan, Hazel (1974) | Professor, Theater |
| Halverson, Stephen P. (1973) | Associate Professor, Early Childhood Education |
| Hamilton, William C. (1973) | Professor, Management |
| Hatfield, Dorothy (1958) | Associate Professor, Director, English |
| Henderson, Bob G. (1975) | Professor, Educational Foundations |
| Henderson, Malcolm (1970) | Professor, Finance |
| *Holmes, Joel H. (1983) | Associate Professor, Library |
| Howell, Robert S. (1961) | Associate Professor, Finance |
| Johnson, David J. (1966) | Professor, English |
| Joy, Arthur C. Jr. (1991) | Associate Professor, Accounting |
| Justice Sr., Arthur E. (1989) | Professor, Educational Administration and Supervision |
| Kao, Charles Tsun-Hsiung (1967) | Professor, Physics |
| Klein, Ronald D. (1974) | Professor, Management |
| Kundey, Gary E. (1974) | Professor, Finance |
| Land, Arthur J. (1971) | Professor, Educational Administration |
| *Lee, Virginia C. (1961) | Associate Professor, Library Science |
| LeNoir, William C. (1960) | Professor, Dean, Botany |
| Lindquist, Mary M. (1984) | Callaway Professor, Mathematics Education |
| *Livengood, Mary L. (1958) | Registrar, Student Services |
| Lloyd, Craig (1971) | Professor, History |
| Lumley, J. Kitt (1977) | Professor, Mathematics |
| Lupold, John S. (1970) | Professor, Chair, History |

| | |
|---|---|
| McCollum, James B. (1976) | Professor, Economics |
| McGee, Billy D. (1964) | Associate Professor, History |
| *McLendon, Alvin (1958) | Professor, Physical Science |
| *Milian, Helen T. (1967) | Professor, Chair, Nursing |
| Mion, Mario R. (1975) | Professor, Political Science |
| Mitchell-Tibbs, Marlene P. (1983) | Professor, Director, Nursing |
| Mock, W. Lindsey (1961) | Vice President, Student Affairs |
| Murzyn, John S. (1970) | Professor, History |
| Myers, John B. (1970) | Professor, History |
| *Nance, Kenneth (1958) | Professor, Biology |
| *Parker, Charles A. (1969) | Professor, Education |
| *Petlewski, Paul J. (1971) | Associate Professor, English |
| Phelps, Ferinez B. (1970) | Professor, Political Science |
| Ragsdale, Charles F. (1965) | Professor, Physical Education and Recreation |
| Riggsby, Ernest D. (1969) | Professor, Science Education |
| Robinson, Thelma M. (1970) | Counselor, Counseling and Placement |
| Rodgers, Hugh I. (1967) | Professor, History |
| *Safar, Milo R. (1971) | Associate Professor, Program Director, Dental Hygiene |
| *Sanders, James O. (1961) | Vice President, Business and Finance |
| Scanling, Frederick H. (1967) | Associate Professor, Management |
| *Sears, Robert L. (1969) | Professor, Education |
| Spano, Patricia A. (1967) | Associate Professor, English |
| Stanback, Rosa S. (1970) | Professor, Social Science Education. |
| Stewart, Jack C. (1972) | Professor Educational Foundations |
| Stinson, Gerald L. (1974) | Associate Professor, Mathematics |
| Taylor, Earlene P. (1970) | Professor, Accounting |
| Taylor, Michaell K. (1976) | Professor, Physical Education and Leisure Management |
| Thomas, John J. (1974) | Professor, Philosophy |
| Trigg, Rodger R. (1975) | Professor, Accounting |
| VanCleave, Jr., Albert R. (1971) | Professor, Mathematics |
| Voynich, John J. (1969) | Professor, Management |
| Wabo, Sister Mary Ann (1971) | Associate Professor, Nursing |
| Wadkins, Mary J. (1971) | Associate Professor, History |

| | |
|---|---|
| Walls, Glen D. (1973) | Professor, Educational Psychology |
| *Webb, Joe S. (1968) | Professor, Criminal Justice |
| Wentland, Thomas J. (1979) | Professor, Communicative Disorders |
| *Whitley, Thomas Y. (1958) | President, Education |
| Whitman, Anita. B. (1974) | Professor, Elementary Education |
| Whitman, Harold L. (1969) | Professor, Reading Education |
| Yates, Jerrel K. (1976) | Professor, Mathematics/Computer Science |
| Zheng, Quan (2006) | Temporary Assistant Professor, Mathematics |
| Zimmerly, Belle M. (1980) | Associate Professor, Marketing |

*Deceased

# Index

Adams, George 13

Aflac 87, 103

Agnew, Mike 45

Allen, J.R. 53

Alumni Gateway 51-53

Anderson, John E. 51, 58-59

Appleton, Greg 95

Archives 8-9, 64-65, 73

Armon, Larry 21

Armon, Lowell 21

Arnold Building 37

Arnold, Robert M. 11-12, 37

Arnold, Robert O. 19

Athletic Hall of Fame 93

Austin, Thomas 76

Banks, Pauline C. 110

Baptist Student Union 24, 105

Barr, Robert M. 33

Baseball team 25-26, 67-68, 93, 95

Basketball team 20-21, 25-26, 30, 46, 48, 58, 61-62, 67, 93-95, 107

Battiato, Brinson 26

Battle, Mrs. Willis 11

Battle, Philip 10, 17, 24, 110

Bed races 54

Belknap Robert 22, 28

Berry, Arthur N. 41

Betts, Adelaide 20-21, 111

Bickerstaff, Richard H. 41

Biggs, Alfonso 73

Black Applause Banquet 67

Black Student Union 46-47

Blackmon, Mary V. 25-26

Blackwell, Mike 56

Blanchard, James W. 41

Blount, Jimmy 28

Bonachea, Rolanda 76

Born, Clifford 27

Bowers, Sr., Lloyd 14

Bradley, Forbes 15

Bradley, Mrs. Forbes 13

Bradley-Turner Foundation 99

Branson, Doug 95

Briley, Jr., A.C. 15

Brinkley, Jack 73, 117

Britton, Cliff 45

Broadway Crossing 103

Brogdon, Bill 26, 28

Brooke, Francis J. 58, 60-64, 66, 68-71, 73, 76, 108

Brostrom, Teddy 21

Brown, Etta 28

Brown, Frank Douglas 6-7, 9, 60-61, 74, 76-78, 88, 96, 103-105, 117

Brown, Wimberly 110, 117, 119

Bryan, Jr., Morris M. 19

Buck, Jr., Thomas 41

Buck, William 15

Burnett, Robert 21, 26

Byars, Jim 42-43

Caldwell, Harmon W. 19, 33

Callaway, Howard "Bo" 15, 19-20, 56

Callaway, Jr., Cason 41

Callihan, Inman 26

Camera Club 24

Carr, Nancy 57, 115

Carr, Virginia Spencer 69, 112

Carson McCullers Center for Writers and Musicians 99

Carter, Jimmy 56

Cash, Dewey 26, 29, 110, 119

Casion, George 26

Center for Commerce and Technology 106

Center for Excellence in Science and Education 82

Center for International Education 88

Chai, Nemia 117, 119

Chaplin, Mrs. Richard 13

Chappell, William 114, 117

Charting a New Course for Business and Education (COMPASS) 85-87

Cheerleading 22, 93, 96

Choir 33

Choral Readers 57

Clements, Frank "Sonny" 25-26, 30, 58, 61-62, 67, 119

Clemmons, Bill 28

Cobos, Patricio 67

Coca-Cola Space Science Center 82, 85, 103

Cole, Bobby 29
Columbus College Alumni Association 79-80
Columbus Regional Mathematics Collaborative 82
Columbus Technical College 85
Columbus Water Works 11, 82-83
Comer, J. Wilson 23-24
COMPASS 85-87
Coolik, Sammy 29
Cooper, John 105
Corn Center for the Visual Arts 100, 102
Cosmopolitan Club (see also, Black Student Union) 46-47, 57
Courtyard on College 78-79
Crail, Dale 60, 76
Crowe, Wanda 106
Crowley, Ray E. 66
Crumpler, Ken 29
Cruzen, Shawn 113, 117
Cunningham Center for Leadership Development 100, 103, 107
Cunningham, John 107
Daley, Charles S. 41
Daniel, Roland 11
Davidson Building 37, 49, 54
Davidson, J.Q. 1, 11-13, 15, 19-20, 37-38, 41
Davis, Jimbo 96
Davis, Robert T. 15

Debate team 57
Dewberry, J.H. 19, 33
Dezendolet, Sue A. 60-61, 63, 69-70
Dillard, Doyle M. 110
Dillard, Guy 13
Dison, Peanut 26
Dixon, Robert 46
Dozier, Gary 48
Dramatics club 20
Duncan, Rosemary 110
Dyess, Carol 28
Eason, Charles 51, 116, 117
Edmondson, James 28
Eisiminger, Sterling 45
Elena Diaz-Verson Amos Eminent Scholar in Latin American Studies 88
Elizabeth Bradley Turner Center for Continuing Education 39, 41
Elmore, Marlene 27, 111
Embry, Olice 63, 70
English Language Institute 88, 90
Entlich, Jay 96
Espada, Jessica 105
Evers, Ralph 53
Faculty Office Building 39
Fant, Ben 26
Fellowship Council 28
Fine Arts Hall 39-41, 66, 72, 76
Florence, Ricky 46

Flowers, Mrs. J. E. 11
Fort Benning 36, 65
Fort, T. Hicks 13
Forte, Malcolm 15
Frank G. Lumpkin, Jr. Center 92-94, 96
Franklin, Billy J. 59
Franklin, Carl 23, 27, 111, 115
Frazier, William 76, 112
Fujino, Hisa 98
Genesis Gospel Choir 97
Gibson, Marilyn 27
Glee Club 20, 24
Glenn, Wilbur H. 15, 41
Golf team 26, 29, 67, 93, 96
Goodroe, Brenda 28
Goodroe, Susan 22, 28
Gore, Jr., Al 85-87
Green, Lavern 22
Greene, Herbert 61-62, 67-68, 95
Greentree, Myron 41
Greer, Nicholas 98
Grey and Gold (see also, Sentry) 8, 27
Griffin, Marvin 15-16
Grimes, Judy 23, 111
Hadley, Linda 116, 118
Hamrick, Don 26
Harbuck, Don 51
Harbuck, Judy 22
Hardaway, III, B.H. 41
Hardaway, Jr., B.H. 13, 15, 33

Hare, Marquis 98
Hatcher, Mrs. J. Madden 13
Hawkins, John 56
Hayes, Hubert 26
Hegarty, Thomas 76
Herrin, Glen 10, 110
Hobbes, Mrs. Ralph 41
Hollis, Howell 41-42
Hollis, W. Slater 60
Holmes, Lamar 26
Holmes, Maria 106
Homecoming 54, 57
Howard Hall 31, 36, 49, 79
Howard, William 24, 28, 36, 110
Hunter, Elizabeth 28
Hutchins, Beth 28
IBM 61, 85
ICAPP 85-87
Illges Health Science Building 38-39, 72
Illges, John P. 38
Illges, Jr., Mrs. J.P. 4
Intellectual Capital Partnership Program 86
International House 88
Intramural council 26
IPTAY-ettes 55
Isaacs, MacAllister 42
J. Kyle and Sara D. Spencer Charitable
    Trust 88
Jackson, Harry C. 41, 125
Jenkins, Don 21-22

Jenkins, Wimberley 11
Johnson, Arlene 76
Johnson, John 28
Johnson, Joseph C. 63
Johnson, Mary Hill 118
Jones, Carolyn 22
Jones, J. Stacey 13
Jones, Thomas Z. 77
Jordan Hall 39, 72, 79
Jordan High School 10, 14
Jordan II, G. Gunby 41
Jordan Vocational High School Band 33
Jordan, Walter 26, 28
Junior College Act of 1958 16
Junior College Study Report 14, 16
Kelly, Charles 26
Kendrick, Ms. T.K. 41
Key, Jack B. 12
Kinchen, Ray 29
King, Arleen 28
Kinnett, John 11, 13
Kinnett, Sr., John R. 15, 33, 41
Kirkpatrick, Eleanor 27
Kiryu Garden 88, 90
Kite, Wallace 80, 116
Kunze, Louis 13
Lakes, Ray 3, 9, 57
Lambda Iota Tau 57
Lammons, Eddie 26
Landrum, Jr., Hugh 66

Lane, James 21, 26, 111
Langford, Nancy 27, 111
Lawson, Jo Ann 27
Learning Center and Tutorial Program 42
Ledford, Bobby 28
Lee, Harper 25
LeNoir Hall 29, 78
LeNoir, Jr., William C. 24, 29, 59, 63, 76,
    78, 120
Lewis, Hazel 35
Lindquist, Mary 113, 117, 120
Livengood, Mary L. 17, 28, 70, 110, 120
Lloyd, Craig 8-9, 40, 42-43, 64-66,
    108-109, 113, 120
Loughman, Tom 57, 114
Loureiro, Lucus 116, 118
Lumpkin, Jr., Frank 93
Lupold, John S. 3, 8-9, 11, 64, 109,
    113-114, 118, 120
Maddox, Mary 22
Mahan, Katherine B. 17, 24, 29, 33, 110
Mann, Derek 67
Marlowe, Lon 9, 57, 60, 76, 115
Martin, Carolyn 28, 115
Martin, Jr., R.E. 15
May, Sharon 106
McClung, Curtis 49
McClure, Charles A. 66
McCrillis, Neal 88
McDowell, Richard E. 59-60

McGee, Billy 112, 117, 121

McGee, Theodore J. 11

McLendon, Alvin 28, 110, 121

Melvin, Carson 27

Mercer, Susan 115, 117

Mergler, Wayne 45

Mildred Miller Fort Foundation
    Distinguished Chair of International
    Education 88

Mildred Miller Fort Visiting Scholar in
    European Studies 88

Miller Dairy 12, 14, 16, 30, 51

Miller, Walter L. 12

Mion, Anna 116-117

Miss Columbus College 28, 57

Miss Saber 20-21

Miss Sentry 57

Mock, Lindsey 3, 9, 32, 45, 52, 60, 76,
    121

Moon, Clinton 11

Moon, W.H. 13

Moore, Mary 27, 111

Moore, Thomas G. 15

Morrow, Pete 42

Morton, Lucius 56

Munford, Wade 21, 26, 111

Munro, Paul 11

Music Library 70, 96, 99

Nance, Kenneth 17, 110, 121

Neal, Kendust & Murray 80

Nelson, Jim 21

Noles, David 62

Orchestra 74

Oxbow Meadows Environmental Learning
    Center 82-84, 103

Parkman, Melanie 19

Parmer, Norman 59-60

Passailaique, Jack M. 41, 43, 70

Pate, George 26

Pattillo, Charles 76, 78

Paul, Geri 3, 9, 57, 117

Pearce, W. Ford 15

Penson, Merryll S. 73

Peters, Bobby 92

Phillips, Bill 22

Phillips, Frank 15

Pickard, A.M. 15

Pickens, Arthur 53

Portch, Stephen R. 92-93

Porter, Fredrick S. 33

Prather, Andrew 12

Propst, H. Dean 69-70, 74, 76

Pugh, Evelyn Turner 73, 116

Quick, Johnny 28, 115

R.H. Wright, Jr. and Associates 31

Ragsdale Field 96

Ragsdale, Charles 67, 121

Rankin Arts Center 99

Redmond, Patsy 106, 115

Reeves, T.G. 12

Register, B.F. 15

Reynolds, Jack 21

Richards Building/Hall 37, 88, 90

Richards, Walter A. 11-13, 15, 37

Ries, Christian 96

Riley, Marcia 67

RiverCenter for the Performing Arts 70,
    96-99, 103

RiverPark Campus 39, 100, 102-103

Rodgers, Hugh 117, 121

Rodgers, Larry 21

Roe, Lee 27

Rothschild, Jac H. 38

Rothschild, Maurice D. 11-12

Ruggs, Peggy 46

Russell, Alton 19

Ryan, William 28

*Saber 8, 21, 28, 49, 51, 57-58, 61-62, 68,
    70-71, 76, 80, 93, 108, 117*

Sanders, Carl E. 15, 30, 33-35

Sanders, Jim 58, 121

Saunders Center for Music Studies 99

Saunders, Gerald B. 41

Saunders, Martha 107

Schorr, Jack 21

Schuster Student Success Center 100

Schwob, Henry 41

Schwob, Ruth 39-40, 67, 70

Schwob, Simon 39-40

*Sentry* (see also, *Grey and Gold*) 8, 47, 57

Servant Leadership Program 99, 104

Shannon Hosiery Mill 6, 10, 16-19, 23, 27, 32, 77, 79

Shaw, William Henry 11-12, 14-15, 33-35

Simon Schwob Memorial Library 36, 39-40, 71, 73

Skinner, Linda 28

Slayden, Janice 28

Slayton, Jack 21

Smith, Al 21

Smith, Charles 26

Soccer team 96

Sonich, Jerry 29

Soter, Richard P. 59

Spano, Ken 26

Spano, Mrs. Joseph 15

Spano, Patricia 117, 121

Sparks, Jay 94

Spectrum 45

Spence, Richard 40

Spencer High School 45

Spencer House 88-89

Staff Council 106

Stanley Hall 24, 39, 72, 87

Stanley, T. Hiram 15, 23-24, 33

Stanton, George 53, 59-60, 112, 114

Stephens, Gail 28

Streaking 49, 51, 60

Student Government Association 20, 28, 44-46, 56-57, 62, 118

Swift, W.D. 15

Tanner, Roy 43

Tau Kappa Epsilon 55

Taylor, Mike 67

Taylor, Tommy 19

Taylor, Wendell 40

Theatre on the Park 100-102

Thompson, Lois 110

Thompson, Toni 56

Total Systems Services, Inc. (TSYS) 85-87, 103

Tower Society 99

Townsend, Frank 21, 110

Townsend, John 44-45, 67

Treetop Trail 84

Tuck, Rudon 21

Tucker Building 31, 36

Tucker, Sr., William C. 36

Turner, D. Abbott 41, 66

Turner, Elizabeth Bradley 41

Tuttle, Ron 76

University of Georgia Extension Center 14

Vander Gheynst, Paul 63, 112

Volleyball team 26, 55

Wallace, Malcolm 21

Watford, Peggy 10

Welsh, Jimmy 56

Westminster Fellowship 105

Whiddon, Rex 67

Whitley, Mary Jo 51

Whitley, Thomas Y. 10, 16-17, 23-24, 28-29, 33, 40-41, 45-47, 49-53, 58-59, 70, 80, 110, 122

Whitley, Thomas Y., Clock Tower 75, 79-80, 92, 106

Wilkes, Wayne 27

Williams, Charlie Frank 14

Williams, Harry L. 11

Wilson, Margaret 19

Wilson, Mrs. Sam 15

Woodall Building 31

Woodall, Sr., Allen 15, 41

Woodall, W.C. 13

Woodruff Gymnasium 31, 36, 93

Woodruff, George C. 11

Woodruff, Jr., James W. 41

Woodruff, Sr., James W. 36

Yancey Center at One Arsenal Place 102

Yancey, Jimmy 99-100, 116

Young Democrats 56-57

Young Republicans 56

Young, J. Gordon 15

# About the Author | Reagan Grimsley

Reagan L. Grimsley serves as assistant professor of library science and archivist at Columbus State University. He holds a B.S. in history, an M.A. in history, and an M.L.I.S. in library and information science, all from the University of Southern Mississippi, and is currently enrolled in the doctoral program in history at Georgia State University. Before coming to Columbus State in 2001, he served as special collections librarian at Pikeville College in Pikeville, Kentucky.

Mr. Grimsley is the author of the 2004 volume *Hattiesburg in Vintage Postcards,* and also penned *A One Hundred Year History of the First Baptist Church, Sumrall, Mississippi* in 2005. He frequently publishes journal articles in state and regional history and library journals, and serves as the editor of *Provenance: The Journal of the Society of Georgia Archivists* and *Muscogiana: The Journal of the Muscogee Genealogical Society.* In 2006, he was the recipient of the Columbus State University Faculty Research and Scholarship Award.

Reagan L. Grimsley